Adventures in Writing
Implementing the Structure and Style® Method

Teacher's Manual

First Edition © June 2023
Institute for Excellence in Writing, L.L.C.

The purchase of this book allows its owner access to PDF downloads that accompany *Adventures in Writing*. See blue page for details and download instructions. Our duplicating/copying policy for these resources is specified on the copyright page for each of these downloads.

Copyright Policy
Adventures in Writing: Implementing the Structure and Style® Method Teacher's Manual
First Edition, June 2023
Copyright © 2023 Institute for Excellence in Writing

ISBN 978-1-62341-404-7

Our duplicating/copying policy for *Adventures in Writing* Teacher's Manual:

All rights reserved.

No part of this book may be reproduced, stored in a retrieval system, or transmitted in any form or by any means, electronic, mechanical, photocopying, recording, or otherwise, without the prior written permission of the publisher, except as provided by U.S.A. copyright law and the specific policy below:

Home use: Because this Teacher's Manual may not be reproduced, each family must purchase its own copy.

Small group or co-op classes: Because this Teacher's Manual may not be reproduced, each teacher must purchase his or her own copy.

Classroom teachers: Because this Teacher's Manual may not be reproduced, each teacher must purchase his or her own copy.

Library use: This Teacher's Manual may be checked out of a lending library provided patrons agree not make copies.

Additional copies of this Teacher's Manual may be purchased from IEW.com/AIW-T

Institute for Excellence in Writing (IFW®)
8799 N. 387 Road
Locust Grove, OK 74352
800.856.5815
info@IEW.com
IEW.com

Printed in the United States of America

IEW® and Structure and Style® are registered trademarks of the Institute for Excellence in Writing, L.L.C.

Contributors

Sabrina Cardinale
Denise Kelley
Sharyn Staggers
Heidi Thomas
Julie Walker

Designer

Melanie Anderson

Illustrator

Erin Covey

Accessing Your Downloads
Teacher's Manual

The purchase of this book allows its owner access to PDF downloads of the following:

- the optional *Adventures in Writing* Reproducible Checklists
- the optional *Adventures in Writing* Vocabulary Cards
- the optional *Adventures in Writing* Exemplars

To download these e-resources, please follow the directions below:

1. Go to our website: IEW.com
2. Log in to your online customer account. If you do not have an account, you will need to create one.
3. After you are logged in, type this link into your address bar: IEW.com/AIW-TE
4. Click the checkboxes next to the names of the files you wish to place in your account.
5. Click the "Add to my files" button.
6. To access your files now and in the future, click on "Your Account" and click on the "Files" tab (one of the gray tabs).
7. Click on each file name to download the files onto your computer.

Please note: You may download and print these PDF files as needed for use within *your immediate family*. However, this information is proprietary, and we are trusting you to be on your honor not to share it with anyone. Please see the copyright page for further details.

If you have any difficulty receiving these downloads after going through the steps above, please call 800.856.5815.

Institute for Excellence in Writing
8799 N. 387 Road
Locust Grove, OK 74352

Contents

Introduction 5
Scope and Sequence 8

UNIT 1: NOTE MAKING AND OUTLINES
Lesson 1	Nile River, Yangtze River	11
Lesson 2	Roman Hoplite, American Quarter Horse	19
Lesson 3	Orchestra and Conductor	25

UNIT 2: WRITING FROM NOTES
Lesson 4	Roman Colosseum	29
Lesson 5	Tornadoes	37
Lesson 6	Benjamin Franklin's Lightning Rod	45
Lesson 7	Hannibal's War	53

UNIT 3: RETELLING NARRATIVE STORIES
Lesson 8	The Fox and the Crow, Part 1	61
Lesson 9	The Fox and the Crow, Part 2	67
Lesson 10	The Theft of Thor's Hammer, Part 1	73
Lesson 11	The Theft of Thor's Hammer, Part 2	77

UNIT 4: SUMMARIZING A REFERENCE
Lesson 12	Leif Eriksson	83
Lesson 13	Hagia Sophia	93
Lesson 14	John Muir	101
Lesson 15	Magnets	109
Lesson 16	Dolphins	119

UNIT 5: WRITING FROM PICTURES
Lesson 17	Rooster, Part 1	127
Lesson 18	Rooster, Part 2	133
Lesson 19	Treasure Map, Part 1	139
Lesson 20	Treasure Map, Part 2	143

UNIT 6: SUMMARIZING MULTIPLE REFERENCES
Lesson 21	Roanoke, Part 1	149
Lesson 22	Roanoke, Part 2	157
Lesson 23	Mayflower, Part 1	163
Lesson 24	Mayflower, Part 2	173
Lesson 25	William Penn, Part 1	179
Lesson 26	William Penn, Part 2	189

UNIT 7: INVENTIVE WRITING

    Lesson 27   My House, Part 1 195
    Lesson 28   My House, Part 2 201
    Lesson 29   My Friend, Part 1 207
    Lesson 30   My Friend, Part 2 213

Appendices

    I.   Adding Literature 221
    II.   Mechanics 223
    III.   Vocabulary 225
    IV.   Review Games (Teacher's Manual only) 241

Welcome to *Adventures in Writing*. This Teacher's Manual shows reduced copies of the Student Book pages along with instructions to teachers and sample key word outlines. Please be aware that this manual is not an answer key. The samples provided in this book are simply possibilities of what you and your students could create.

Lesson instructions are directed to the student, but teachers should read them over with their students and help as necessary, especially with outlining and structure and style practice. It is assumed that teachers have viewed and have access to IEW's *Teaching Writing: Structure and Style* video course and own the *Seminar Workbook*. Before each new unit, teachers should review the appropriate information in that workbook and video. You can find references to the *Teaching Writing: Structure and Style* course in the teacher's notes for each new unit.

Introduction

The lessons in this book teach Structure and Style® in writing. As they move through various themes and subjects, they incrementally introduce and review the models of structure and elements of style found in the Institute for Excellence in Writing's *Teaching Writing: Structure and Style®*.

Student Book Contents

- **Scope and Sequence Chart** (pages 8–9)

- **The Lesson Pages**
  This is the majority of the text. It contains the instructions, source texts, worksheets, and checklists you will need for each lesson.

- **Appendix I: Adding Literature**
  This appendix suggests various books and stories to be read or listened to.

- **Appendix II: Mechanics**
  This appendix contains a compilation of the correct mechanics of writing numbers, punctuating dates, referencing individuals, etc. that are found in many of the lessons. Well-written compositions are not only written with structure and style, but they also contain correctly spelled words and proper punctuation.

- **Appendix III: Vocabulary**
  This appendix provides a list of the vocabulary words and their definitions organized by lesson as well as quizzes to take periodically. Twenty-three lessons include new vocabulary words. Every lesson includes vocabulary practice. The goal is that these great words will become part of your natural writing vocabulary.

  Vocabulary cards are found on the blue page as a PDF download. Print them, cut them out, and place them in a plastic bag or pencil pouch for easy reference. Plan to study the words for the current lesson and continue to review words from previous lessons.

Customizing the Checklist

The total point value of each assignment is indicated at the bottom of each checklist. This total reflects only the basic items and does not include the vocabulary words. If vocabulary words are included, add the appropriate amount of points and write the new total on the custom total line.

Important: Teachers and parents should remember IEW's EZ+1 Rule when introducing IEW stylistic techniques. The checklist should include only those elements of style that have become easy plus one new element. If students are not yet ready for a basic element on the checklist, simply have them cross it out. Subtract its point value from the total possible and write the new total on the custom total line at the bottom. If you would like to add elements to the checklist, assign each a point value and add these points to the total possible, placing the new total on the custom total line.

Reproducible checklists are available. See the blue page for download information.

Checklists

Each writing lesson includes a checklist that details all the requirements of the assignment. Tear the checklist out of the book so that you can use it while writing. Check off each element when you are sure it is included in your paper. With each writing assignment, turn in the checklist to be used by the teacher for grading. Reproducible checklists are available. See the blue page for download information.

Teacher's Manual

The Teacher's Manual includes all of the Student Book contents with added instructions for teachers, including sample key word outlines and style practice ideas. Teachers may teach directly from this manual without the need of their own copy of the Student Book.

Teaching Writing: Structure and Style

Along with the accompanying Teacher's Manual for this Student Book, it is required that the teacher of this course has access to *Teaching Writing: Structure and Style*. This product is available in DVD format or Forever Streaming. For more information, please visit IEW.com/TWSS

Adapting the Schedule

Groups who follow a schedule with fewer than thirty weeks will have to omit some lessons. Because there are several lessons for each of the seven IEW units in this book, this is not a problem. Teach lessons that introduce new concepts and omit some of those that do not.

Grading with the Checklist

To use the checklists for grading, do not add all the points earned. Instead, if an element is present, put a check in the blank across from it. If an element is missing, write the negative point value on its line. Total the negative points and subtract them from the total possible (or your custom total).

Note: Students should have checked the boxes in front of each element they completed.

Encourage students to bring a thesaurus to class. Most students enjoy using an electronic thesaurus, but for those who prefer books, IEW offers a unique one entitled *A Word Write Now*.

This schedule is provided to emphasize to parents and students, particularly in a class setting, that teachers and students should not expect to complete an entire lesson in one day. Spreading work throughout the week will produce much better writing with much less stress. Parents teaching their own children at home should follow a similar schedule.

Assignment Schedule

All of the instructions for what to do for each lesson are included in the Assignment Schedule located on the first page of each lesson. Each lesson is divided into four days of instruction.

Some writing assignments are divided into two parts, allowing students two lessons to complete the entire assignment. Part one focuses on structure and writing a key word outline. Part two focuses on style and writing the paragraph(s).

Students will benefit from learning new structure and style concepts with a teacher. In addition, students should plan to read the source texts and begin key word outlines with a teacher.

Scope and Sequence

Lesson	Subject and Structure	Style (First Introduced)	Vocabulary Words
Unit 1 1	Nile River, Yangtze River introduction to structure		dwell vast
2	Roman Hoplite American Quarter Horse		organized sprint
3	Orchestra and Conductor		melodious observe
Unit 2 4	Roman Colosseum		
5	Tornadoes	introduction to style -ly adverb	abruptly forcefully
6	Benjamin Franklin's Lightning Rod title rule		cautiously cleverly
7	Hannibal's War	*who/which* clause	guide terrified
Unit 3 8	The Fox and the Crow, Part 1		crave sly
9	The Fox and the Crow, Part 2		
10	The Theft of Thor's Hammer, Part 1		desperately vanish
11	The Theft of Thor's Hammer, Part 2	strong verb banned words: *say/said*	deceive declare
Unit 4 12	Leif Eriksson topic-clincher sentences	banned words: *see/saw*	abundantly notice
13	Hagia Sophia		colossal proudly
14	John Muir	banned words: *go/went*	
15	Magnets	*because* clause	effortlessly metallic

Lesson	Subject and Structure	Style (First Introduced)	Vocabulary Words
16	Dolphins		mottled tussle
Unit 5 17	Rooster, Part 1		commotion slumber
18	Rooster, Part 2		din peacefully
19	Treasure Map, Part 1		
20	Treasure Map, Part 2	quality adjective banned words: *good, bad*	delicate discover
Unit 6 21	Roanoke, Part 1 source and fused outlines		skilled weir
22	Roanoke, Part 2		construct nutritious
23	Mayflower, Part 1		cramped shiver
24	Mayflower, Part 2	*www.asia* clause	
25	William Penn, Part 1		expel illegal
26	William Penn, Part 2		design desire
Unit 7 27	My House, Part 1		bond store
28	My House, Part 2		comfortable spacious
29	My Friend, Part 1		
30	My Friend, Part 2		

Adventures in Writing: Student Book

Lesson 1: Nile River, Yangtze River

Preparation: *Teaching Writing: Structure and Style*
Watch the sections for Unit 1: Note Making and Outlines.
At IEW.com/twss-help reference the TWSS Viewing Guides.

Structure: Unit 1: Note Making and Outlines
Introduction to Structure

Subject: Nile River, Yangtze River

UNIT 1: NOTE MAKING AND OUTLINES

Lesson 1: Nile River, Yangtze River

Goals

- to learn the Unit 1 Note Making and Outlines structural model
- to create a key word outline (KWO)
- to retell the content of a source text using just your outline
- to use new vocabulary words: *dwell, vast*

Assignment Schedule

Day 1

1. Read Introduction to Structure and New Structure.
2. Read and discuss the source text "Nile River."
3. Reread the source text one sentence at a time and circle two or three key words that tell the sentence's main idea.
4. Write your key word outline (KWO) by copying the key words onto the outline. Use symbols, numbers, and abbreviations when possible.
5. Test your KWO. If a note is unclear, check the source text and fix your KWO.

Day 2

1. Look at the vocabulary cards for Lesson 1. Complete Vocabulary Practice.
2. Try to add one vocabulary word to your KWO.
3. Give an oral report using your KWO. Read. Think. Look up. Speak.

Day 3

1. Read and discuss "Endangered Species of the Yangtze River."
2. Reread the source text one sentence at a time and circle two or three key words that tell the sentence's main idea.
3. Write your KWO.
4. Try to add one vocabulary word to your KWO.
5. Test your KWO. If a note is unclear, check the source text and fix your KWO.

Unit 1

Students will benefit from reading the source text and beginning KWOs with a teacher. Teachers should plan to teach New Structure, New Style, and introduce the vocabulary words.

Adventures in Writing: Student Book

UNIT 1: NOTE MAKING AND OUTLINES

Day 4

1. Review the vocabulary words and their meanings.

2. After practicing, use one of your KWOs to give an oral report to a friend or family member. Read. Think. Look up. Speak. If applicable, be prepared to give an oral report in class.

Literature Suggestions

If you wish to incorporate literature into the curriculum, see a suggested list of books in Appendix I.

Introduction to Structure

In this book you will learn to write with *structure* and with *style*.
This lesson explains structure.

Structure

What is structure? The dictionary says structure is "the way that parts of something are arranged or put together."

What has structure? Think of a castle. Before the castle was built, someone had to draw plans for the builders. The builders had to follow the plans so that each part of the castle was in its proper place. The royal family would not have wanted a dungeon next to the bedrooms. Each part had to be placed in its own special spot. Each step had to be completed in order to give the castle its proper structure.

In some ways, writing a paper is similar to building a castle. A paper contains facts and ideas. If you begin writing without a plan, your facts and ideas will probably end up in the wrong place. Your paragraph will not be structured well, and your readers might not understand what you are trying to say. So, in this course you will "draw plans" before you write. Your "plans" will be key word outlines, which we abbreviate KWO.

Lesson 1: Nile River, Yangtze River

New Structure

Note Making and Outlines

Begin by reading the source text. Choose two or three key words in each sentence that tell the sentence's main idea. Circle the words.

To write a key word outline (KWO), place the key words on the outline. Do not write more than three words on a line. You may also use symbols, numbers, and abbreviations. They are "free." Separate key words, symbols, numbers, and abbreviations with commas.

Key words	are the most important words that tell the main idea.
Symbols	can be drawn faster than it takes to write the word.
Numbers	include numerals like 1, 2, 3, and 1st, 2nd, 3rd.
Abbreviations	are commonly accepted forms of shortened words.

Can you guess what each of the following mean?

After you finish writing your KWO, you must test it. To test a KWO, begin by putting the source text away. Use only your notes. If a note is unclear, check the source text and fix your KWO.

Read	a line of notes.
Think	of a sentence.
Look up	so your eyes are not on the paper.
Speak	in complete sentences. With practice, you can use your KWO to give an oral report about a source text.

Adventures in Writing: Student Book

Encourage students to use symbols, numbers, and abbreviations.
A symbol is legal if it can be written in less time than it takes to write the word.

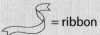

Symbols ⛵ = ship ➔ = to/across/next ∽ = ribbon ++ = many/more/several

Numbers 123 = numbers

Abbreviations ppl = people N↑ = north

UNIT 1: NOTE MAKING AND OUTLINES

Source Text

Read and Discuss

As you read the source text, define words students may not know.

Show students where Africa is located on a map.

Trace the Nile River from Lake Victoria to the Mediterranean Sea and explain how it would look from space.

Locate Key Words

Model how to find key words. Reread the first sentence. Ask your students what words are main idea words. The words chosen for this sample are *Africa*, *longest*, *world*; however, the students may pick *Africa*, *longest*, *river*.

Have students circle two or three key words in each sentence of the source text.

Sentence by sentence, repeat the process by questioning and circling as the students give key word suggestions.

Nile River

The Nile River in (Africa) is the (longest) river in the (world.) It begins in the rivers that flow into (Lake Victoria,) and it empties into the (Mediterranean Sea.) It flows (north) through or along (ten) (countries.) Every year (floods) deposit dirt and fine sand, called (silt,) in the (soil) along the sides of the river. This (silt) helps the (plants) (thrive.) From (space) the Nile looks like a green (ribbon) against the (Sahara Desert.) Many people (depend) on it for (farming,) (transportation,) and electricity.

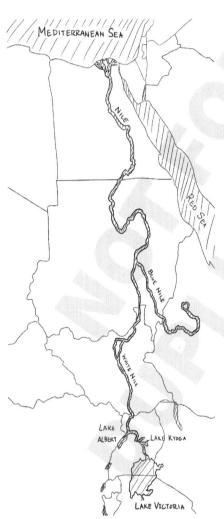

Mechanics

Capitalize proper nouns.

The KWOs in the Teacher's Manual are only samples. Every class and each student will have unique outlines.

Sample

Lesson 1: Nile River, Yangtze River

Key Word Outline

Did you circle two or three key words in each sentence of the source text? On the lines below, write two or three key words from each sentence of "Nile River." Use symbols, numbers, and abbreviations when possible. There is one line for each sentence.

1. NR, Africa, longest, world

2. Lake Victoria → Mediterranean Sea

3. N↑, along, 10, countries

4. floods, silt, soil

5. silt, plants, thrive

6. space, N, 🐍, Sahara Desert

7. ++, depend, farming, transportation

Test your KWO. This is a test of the outline, not your memory.
To test your KWO, look at your notes, not the source text. If a note is unclear, check the source text and fix your KWO.

Read	a line of notes.
Think	of a sentence.
Look up	so your eyes are not on the paper.
Speak	in complete sentences.

Writing the KWO

Symbols, numbers, and abbreviations are free. Using them allows room for other key words.

Since *Nile River* is the title, when forming the KWO simply write *NR*.

Proper nouns such as *Lake Victoria*, *Mediterranean Sea*, and *Sahara Desert* count as one key word. Encourage students to correctly capitalize and spell these words as they write their KWOs.

In a classroom setting, write class ideas on a whiteboard. Students may copy these or use their own ideas.

Tell Back

Telling back the KWO is an important step in the prewriting process.

Adventures in Writing: Student Book

UNIT 1: NOTE MAKING AND OUTLINES

Source Text

Endangered Species of the Yangtze River

The Yangtze River is home to (three) of the world's most (endangered) species of (animals). This river in (China) is the (world's) (third-longest) river. The black and white giant (panda) lives in the (bamboo) (forests) around the upper Yangtze River. Finless (porpoises) dodge (boat) (traffic) in the river. The Yangtze giant (softshell) (turtle) lives in the lower Yangtze River (floodplain). It is (nearly) (extinct). Almost a (thousand) species of other (animals) also call this river (home).

Read and Discuss

Define *endangered* and *species*.

Show students where China and the Yangtze River are located on a map.

Locate Key Words

Reread the first sentence. Ask your students, "If I want to remember the main idea of that sentence, what three words are key words?" The words chosen for this sample are *three, endangered, animals*; however, the students may pick other words.

For instance, *home, endangered, species* would also work.

Sentence by sentence, repeat the process by questioning and circling as the students give key word suggestions.

Sample

Lesson 1: Nile River, Yangtze River

Key Word Outline

Did you circle two or three key words in each sentence? On the lines below, write two or three key words from each sentence of "Endangered Species of the Yangtze River." Use symbols, numbers, and abbreviations when possible. There is one line for each sentence.

1. YR, 3, ++ endangered, animals

2. China, 3rd, longest, R, world

3. g. panda, bamboo, forests, ↑ YR

4. finless porpoises, ⛵, traffic, R

5. Y softshell, turtle, floodplain

6. nearly, extinct

7. 1000, animals, home

Test your KWO. Remember, this is a test of the outline, not your memory. To test your KWO, look at your notes, not the source text. If a note is unclear, check the source text and fix your KWO.

    Read   a line of notes.
    Think   of a sentence.
    Look up   so your eyes are not on the paper.
    Speak   in complete sentences.

Reminder

Symbols, numbers, and abbreviations are free. Using them allows room for other key words.

Train students to use numerals on the KWO. Numerals are always faster than spelling the word.

Tell Back

Telling back the KWO is an important step in the prewriting process.
    Read.
    Think.
    Look up.
    Speak.

Andrew Pudewa teaches, "You may look at your notes, and you may speak to your audience, but you may not do both at the same time."

UNIT 1: NOTE MAKING AND OUTLINES

Vocabulary Practice

Listen   to someone read the vocabulary words for Lesson 1 aloud.

Speak   them aloud yourself.

Read   the definitions and sample sentences on the vocabulary cards.

Write   two sentences using one of this lesson's vocabulary words in each sentence. You may use derivatives of the words. For example, you may add an -ed, -s, or -ing to a basic vocabulary word.

dwell

The giant panda dwells in the bamboo forests near the upper Yangtze River.

vast

The Nile River flows through the vast Sahara Desert.

Think   about the words. Can you use them in your KWOs?

Vocabulary

Students study vocabulary to become better thinkers, speakers, and writers.

Print the vocabulary cards for Lesson 1. Hold up the cards. Read each definition and ask your students to guess which word it matches by looking at the pictures.

Allow students to use derivatives (forms) of words.

The sample sentences are, of course, only suggestions. If students ask for help, offer an idea. Listen as they read their sentences aloud.

Lesson 2: Roman Hoplite, American Quarter Horse

Structure: Unit 1: Note Making and Outlines

Subject: Roman hoplite, American Quarter Horse

UNIT 1: NOTE MAKING AND OUTLINES

Lesson 2: Roman Hoplite, American Quarter Horse

Goals

- to practice the Unit 1 structural model
- to create a key word outline (KWO)
- to use new vocabulary words: *organized, sprint*

Assignment Schedule

Day 1

1. Play Build-a-Man. Directions for this game and other games can be found in the Teacher's Manual.
2. Review Introduction to Structure and New Structure in Lesson 1.
3. Read and discuss "Roman Hoplite."
4. Reread the source text and circle two or three key words in each sentence. Remember, the key words are words that tell the main idea of the sentence.
5. Write your KWO and then test it.

Day 2

1. Look at the vocabulary cards for Lesson 2. Complete Vocabulary Practice.
2. Try to add one vocabulary word to your KWO.
3. Give an oral report using your KWO. Read. Think. Look up. Speak.

Day 3

1. Read and discuss "American Quarter Horse."
2. Reread the source text and circle two or three key words in each sentence.
3. Write your KWO and then test it.

Day 4

1. Review the vocabulary words and their meanings.
2. After practicing, use your KWO and give an oral report to a friend or family member. Read. Think. Look up. Speak. If applicable, be prepared to give an oral report in class.

Build-a-Man

See Appendix IV for game directions. For this lesson use the following phrases and bonus questions.

VERY GREAT IN SIZE
Bonus: What is the vocabulary word? *vast*

THREE KEY WORDS
Bonus: In addition to two or three key words, what may you write on each line of a KWO? *symbols, numbers,* and *abbreviations*

Adventures in Writing: Student Book

UNIT 1: NOTE MAKING AND OUTLINES

Source Text

Roman Hoplite

The hoplite was a foot soldier in the Roman army. He wore heavy armor and carried a large round shield. During battle hoplites fought with swords and spears. Hoplites marched in a formation called a phalanx. This was a tightly packed group of soldiers six to eight men deep. For defense they interlocked their shields. Working together, the hoplites were able to break through the enemy's lines successfully.

Mechanics

Capitalize proper adjectives.

Read and Discuss

Read each source text with your students and ask questions to get them thinking about the information they will be working with. It is also important to make sure students understand words in the text that may be unfamiliar to them.

Locate Key Words

With each source text, model how to find key words. Reread the first sentence. Ask your students, "If I want to remember the main idea of that sentence, what three words are key words?" (Circle those words.)

Encourage students to give suggestions.

Sample

Lesson 2: Roman Hoplite, American Quarter Horse

Key Word Outline

Did you circle two or three key words in each sentence of the source text? On the lines below, write your KWO. Use symbols, numbers, and abbreviations when possible. There is one line for each sentence.

1. H, 👣 soldier, Roman army

2. heavy, armor, large ◎

3. H, battle, swords + spears

4. H, marched, formation, phalanx

5. group, soldiers, 6–8, 👥, deep

6. defense, interlocked, ◎◎

7. together, break, enemy, ╱╱ ║

> *Reminder*
>
> Symbols, numbers, and abbreviations are free. Using them allows room for other key words.
>
> Symbols are not pictures. Symbols save time. They can be drawn faster than it takes to write the word.

Test your KWO. If a note is unclear, check the source text and fix your KWO.

Read   a line of notes.
Think   of a sentence.
Look up so your eyes are not on the paper.
Speak   in complete sentences.

Is it becoming easier for you to retell your notes to someone?

Read and Discuss

Discuss how long a quarter of a mile is. Quarter Horses can run this distance in twenty-one seconds.

Locate Key Words

Sentence by sentence, find and circle key words.

Source Text

American Quarter Horse

The American Quarter Horse is a cross between Spanish and English horses. These horses can run up to fifty-five miles per hour for short distances. Because they can run a quarter of a mile faster than other breeds, they are called Quarter Horses. Farmers and ranchers like Quarter Horses because they can stop suddenly and turn quickly. These motions are helpful for herding cattle. The American Quarter Horse is the most popular horse breed in the United States.

Sample

Key Word Outline

After you have circled two or three key words in each sentence, write your KWO.

1. _Am 1/4 horse = Spanish + English_

2. _run, 55 mph, short, distances_

3. _1/4 horse, 1/4 mi, faster, breeds_

4. _ranchers, ☺, stop, quickly_

5. _helpful, herding, cattle_

6. _Am 1/4 horse, ++ popular, breed, US_

Test your KWO. If a note is unclear, check the source text and fix your KWO.

Read   a line of notes.
Think   of a sentence.
Look up   so your eyes are not on the paper.
Speak   in complete sentences.

Tell Back

Require students to use the KWO to tell back the source text in complete sentences.

Help as needed.

Vocabulary

Help students find a way to use *organized* when telling back the first KWO and *sprint* when telling back the second KWO.

Encouraging students to use new words expands their vocabulary.

UNIT 1: NOTE MAKING AND OUTLINES

Vocabulary Practice

Listen   to someone read the vocabulary words for Lesson 2 aloud.

Speak   them aloud yourself.

Read   the definitions and sample sentences on the vocabulary cards.

Write   the part of speech and the definition beside the word.

 organized

adjective; arranged or planned in an effective way

 sprint

verb; to run very fast for a short distance

Think   about the words. Can you use them in your KWOs?

Lesson 3: Orchestra and Conductor

Structure: Unit 1: Note Making and Outlines
Subject: orchestra and conductor

UNIT 1: NOTE MAKING AND OUTLINES

Lesson 3: Orchestra and Conductor

Goals

- to practice the Unit 1 structural model
- to create a 2-paragraph KWO
- to use new vocabulary words: *melodious, observe*

Assignment Schedule

Day 1

1. Read and discuss "Orchestra and Conductor."
2. Reread the first paragraph of the source text and circle two or three key words in each sentence.
3. Write your KWO for the first paragraph.
4. Test your KWO. Read. Think. Look up. Speak.

Day 2

1. Read and discuss "Orchestra and Conductor" again.
2. Reread the second paragraph of the source text and circle two or three key words in each sentence.
3. Write your KWO for the second paragraph.
4. Test your KWO. Read. Think. Look up. Speak.

Day 3

1. Complete Structure Review.
2. Look at the vocabulary cards for Lesson 3. Complete Vocabulary Practice.
3. Try to add at least one vocabulary word to your KWO.
4. Using your KWO, practice giving an oral report.

Day 4

1. Review the vocabulary words and their meanings.
2. After practicing, use your KWO and give an oral report to a friend or family member. Read. Think. Look up. Speak.

Read and Discuss

Discuss the various types of instruments mentioned in the source text: strings, woodwinds, French horns, percussionists.

Locate Key Words

Sentence by sentence, find and circle key words.

Source Text

Orchestra and Conductor

The people who play in an orchestra are seated according to the sound of their instruments. The quiet strings are placed on the front row. With a more powerful sound, the woodwinds and brass sit behind the strings. The French horns are on the right. This helps the sound from their bells to reach the audience. Percussionists stand at the back and the side. The arrangement of the instruments helps to create beautiful music.

The musicians play together by watching the conductor. Conductors lead the musicians with their hands and a baton. They control the speed, volume, and mood of the music. They  may also use facial expressions to guide the orchestra. They can raise their eyebrows, scowl, or smile. A conductor must read many lines of music at one time. The musicians must pay close attention to the conductor.

From now on, each KWO will begin with a Roman numeral. Each Roman numeral represents one paragraph. In Units 1 and 2 the KWOs have one line for each sentence.

Sample

Lesson 3: Orchestra and Conductor

Key Word Outline

The KWO begins with a Roman numeral. Each Roman numeral represents one paragraph. Write the note for the first sentence of the first paragraph next to Roman numeral I.

I. 👤👤 , orchestra, 🪑, sound, instruments

1. quiet, strings, front
2. woodwinds + brass, behind
3. French horns, right
4. sound, bells → audience
5. percussionists, back, side
6. arrangements, instruments, beautiful 🎶

Write the note for the first sentence of the second paragraph next to Roman numeral II.

II. musicians, play, 👀, conductor

1. C, lead, hands, baton
2. control, speed, vol, mood 🎶
3. expressions, guide, orchestra
4. ↑, eyebrows, scowl, ☺
5. C, read, ++ lines 🎶
6. musicians, 👀, attention, C

Test the KWO. Read. Think. Look up. Speak.

Reminder

After writing *conductor* the first time, simply write C.

UNIT 1: NOTE MAKING AND OUTLINES

Structure Review

> *Structure Review*
>
> Key words are the most important words that tell the main idea.
>
> Two or three words can be placed on a KWO line.
>
> Symbols, numbers, and abbreviations are free.
>
> After you write a KWO, you have to test it.

Review page 13. Answer these questions orally.

What is a key word?

How many words can you put on one line of a KWO?

When you write a KWO, what are free?

After you write a KWO, what do you have to do?

Vocabulary Practice

Listen — to someone read the vocabulary words for Lesson 3 aloud.

Speak — them aloud yourself.

Read — the definitions and sample sentences on the vocabulary cards.

Write — the correct words in the blanks. You may use derivatives of the words. For example, you may add an -ed, -s, or -ing to a basic vocabulary word.

The __*melodious*__ sound of the bells reaches the audience.

Musicians __*observe*__ the conductor to play their instruments.

Think — about the words. Can you use them in your KWO?

Lesson 4: Roman Colosseum

Preparation: *Teaching Writing: Structure and Style*
Watch the sections for Unit 2: Writing from Notes.
At IEW.com/twss-help reference the TWSS Viewing Guides.

Structure: Unit 2: Writing from Notes
Subject: Roman Colosseum

UNIT 2: WRITING FROM NOTES

Lesson 4: Roman Colosseum

Goals
- to learn the Unit 2 Writing from Notes structural model
- to write a 1-paragraph summary
- to be introduced to the composition checklist
- to review vocabulary words

Assignment Schedule

Day 1
1. Play Vocabulary Pictionary.
2. Read and discuss "Roman Colosseum."
3. Reread the source text and circle two or three key words in each sentence.
4. Write your KWO and then test it.

Day 2
1. Read New Structure and Mechanics.
2. Review your KWO from Day 1.
3. Begin writing your rough draft. Use your KWO.
4. Look at the checklist. Check each box as you complete each requirement.

Day 3
1. Complete Vocabulary Review.
2. Finish writing your rough draft. Use your KWO and the checklist. If you use vocabulary words, label them with (voc).
3. Turn in your rough draft to your editor with the completed checklist attached. The backs of all checklists are blank so that they can be removed.

Day 4
1. Study for Vocabulary Quiz 1. It will cover words from Lessons 1–3.
2. Write or type a final draft.
3. Paperclip the checklist, final draft, rough draft, and KWO together.

Unit 2

In Unit 2 students use the KWO to write a summary paragraph. As you model writing from the KWO, stress the importance of writing in your own words.

Exemplar

The Exemplars file contains a student's completed assignment for Lesson 4. The Exemplar is for the teacher and not intended to be used by the student.

See the blue page for download instructions.

Read and Discuss

The abbreviation AD stands for *Anno Domini* in Latin. In English, this means "in the year of our Lord."

The words Colosseum and Rome are capitalized because they are proper nouns. Tell students to copy capitalization and spelling when they write their KWO.

Source Text

Roman Colosseum

In AD 80 the Colosseum in Rome opened. To celebrate, the emperor held one hundred days of games in the new stadium. It could hold fifty thousand people. Men fought in hand-to-hand combat. Lions, bears, and hippos battled. At one point the Colosseum floor was filled with water. Ships were used to act out famous Roman sea battles.

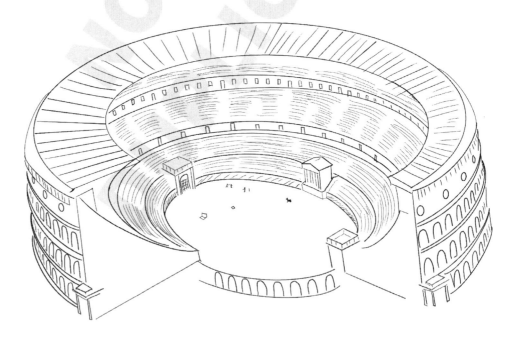

Sample

Lesson 4: Roman Colosseum

Key Word Outline

After you have circled two or three key words in each sentence, write your KWO. Write notes for the first sentence on the Roman numeral line.

I. _____ AD 80, Colosseum, Rome, opened _____

    1. _____ celebrate, emperor, 100 d, games _____

    2. _____ hold, 50,000, people _____

    3. _____ hand-hand, combat _____

    4. _____ lions, bears, battled _____

    5. _____ floor, filled, H_2O _____

    6. _____ ships, act, R, ~~~ , battles _____

Reminder

Symbols, numbers, and abbreviations are free.

Using them allows room for other key words.

d = days

H_2O = water

~~~ = sea

Writing from Notes

Students should write from the KWO. One note may become two or more sentences, or two notes may become one sentence.

What do you do next? Test your KWO!

    Read   a line of notes.

    Think   of a sentence.

    Look up   so your eyes are not on the paper.

    Speak   in complete sentences.

Adventures in Writing: Student Book

UNIT 2: WRITING FROM NOTES

New Structure

Writing from Notes

In Unit 2 you will use your KWO to write a paragraph. You may use your own words, sentences, and ideas.

This is the first sentence of the source text:

In AD 80 the Colosseum in Rome opened.

Your key word notes may look something like this:

I. AD 80, Colosseum, Rome, opened

Practice

Use the key word notes to write a sentence.

Here is an example: In AD 80 the Romans opened the Colosseum.

Answers will vary.

The Editor

You will need to hire an editor to complete your assignments. Your editor will help you with spelling, punctuation, and proper grammar usage. Your editor will also look at the checklist and let you know if anything is not complete. When your editor finishes editing your rough draft, talk about the changes you should make. Then use your rough draft and your editor's comments to write a final draft.

Writing from Notes

In Unit 2 students write summary paragraphs. Do not worry if their paragraphs are similar to the source texts. This will change when students advance to other units.

Editing

When editing, Andrew Pudewa says, "Hands on structure, hands off content." Make the paper grammatically legal; however, refrain from meddling with content.

Paper Format

When you begin your assignment, place your name and the date in the top left corner of the first page.

> Your Name
>
> January 1, 2025
>
> Title Centered
>
> Indent the first line of each paragraph half an inch.
>
> Place one space between sentences. Double-space all lines.

Mechanics

Numbers

Use number words and numerals correctly.

Words	numbers expressed in one or two words	*twenty, fifty-three*	
	ordinal numbers	*first, second, third*	
Numerals	numbers that use three or more words	*123*	*204*
	numbers mixed with symbols	*$500*	*40%*
	dates (Do not include st, nd, rd, or th.)	*AD 80* *January 1, 1950*	

Mechanics

The mechanics rules listed in this book follow guidelines provided in *Fix It! Grammar*, which aligns with the *Chicago Manual of Style*.

Games

Around the World and Elimination are quick games. If you have more time, play Vocabulary Find the Card.

The vocabulary words are optional. Do not require students to use vocabulary words in their writing assignments.

Vocabulary Review

Listen   to someone read the vocabulary words for Lessons 1–3 aloud.

Speak   them aloud yourself.

Read   the definitions and sample sentences on the vocabulary cards.

Write   the words that match the definitions.

melodious   sweet-sounding

dwell   to live; to inhabit

observe   to watch carefully

organized   arranged or planned in an effective way

sprint   to run very fast for a short distance

vast   very great in size

Think   about the words and their meanings. Which vocabulary words could you use in your paragraph?

dwell, vast, observe, organized

If you use a vocabulary word in your paragraph, label it by writing (voc) in the left margin or after the sentence.

Before students begin to write, preview the checklist. This ensures that the students understand expectations.

Lesson 4: Roman Colosseum

Unit 2 Composition Checklist
Lesson 4: Roman Colosseum

Writing from Notes

Institute for Excellence in Writing

Name: _____

STRUCTURE
- ☐ name and date in upper left-hand corner ____ 10 pts
- ☐ composition double-spaced ____ 10 pts
- ☐ title centered ____ 10 pts
- ☐ checklist on top, final draft, rough draft, key word outline ____ 10 pts

MECHANICS
- ☐ capitalization ____ 15 pts
- ☐ end marks and punctuation ____ 15 pts
- ☐ complete sentences ____ 15 pts
- ☐ correct spelling ____ 15 pts

VOCABULARY
- ☐ vocabulary words - label *(voc)* in left margin or after sentence

Total: ____ 100 pts
Custom Total: ____ pts

Adventures in Writing: Student Book

Checklist

In each lesson students are directed to give their editors a rough draft with the completed checklist attached. The back sides of all checklists are blank so they can be removed from the Student Book.

Reproducible checklists are included in the downloads that came with this book. See blue page.

The vocabulary words are optional. Do not require students to use vocabulary words in their writing assignments.

Instruct students to tear the checklist out of the book so that they can use it while writing. Train students to check what they do and do what they check.

UNIT 2: WRITING FROM NOTES

Intentionally blank so the checklist can be removed.

Lesson 5: Tornadoes

Structure: Unit 2: Writing from Notes

Style: Introduction to Style
-ly adverb dress-up

Subject: tornadoes

UNIT 2: WRITING FROM NOTES

Lesson 5: Tornadoes

Goals

- to practice the Units 1 and 2 structural models
- to write a 1-paragraph summary
- to add a new dress-up: -ly adverb
- to take Vocabulary Quiz 1
- to use new vocabulary words: *abruptly, forcefully*

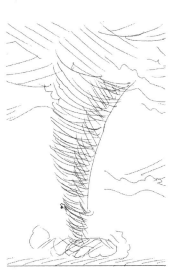

Assignment Schedule

Day 1

1. Play Around the World.
2. Take Vocabulary Quiz 1.
3. Read and discuss "Tornadoes." Circle key words in each sentence.
4. Write your KWO and then test it.

Day 2

1. Review your KWO from Day 1.
2. Read New Style and complete Style Practice.
3. Begin writing your rough draft. Use your KWO.
4. Look at the checklist. Check each box as you complete each requirement.

Day 3

1. Look at the vocabulary cards for Lesson 5. Complete Vocabulary Practice.
2. Finish writing your rough draft. Use your KWO and the checklist. Remember to include and underline one -ly adverb.
3. Turn in your rough draft to your editor with the completed checklist attached.

Day 4

1. Write or type a final draft.
2. Paperclip the checklist, final draft, rough draft, and KWO together.

Motivate

When students turn in their final drafts, read some of their compositions aloud. Clap for them! It motivates writers to hear their pieces being read aloud. This is why we write—for an audience.

Adventures in Writing: Student Book

UNIT 2: WRITING FROM NOTES

Read and Discuss

Throughout this book, students will benefit from reading the source text and beginning KWOs with a teacher.

Source Text

Tornadoes

A tornado is a funnel of air that spins fast. It forms when warm, humid air meets cold, dry air. It stretches from dark thunderclouds all the way to the ground. The tornado picks up dust and debris as it spins. The powerful wind of a tornado can destroy buildings, trees, and bridges. It can even throw cars in the air. The United States has more tornadoes than any other country.

Sample

Lesson 5: Tornadoes

Key Word Outline

After you have circled two or three key words in each sentence, write your KWO. Do you remember what the Roman numeral means? It means that this is the first note of the first paragraph.

I. _____ tornado, 🌪, spins, fast _____

1. _____ forms, warm + cold, 💨 _____

2. _____ thunderclouds, ↓ ground _____

3. _____ ↑ dust + debris, spins _____

4. _____ destroy, 🏠, tree, bridges _____

5. _____ throw, cars ↑ _____

6. _____ US, ++ tornadoes, country _____

Reminder

Symbols are not pictures. Symbols save time. They can be drawn faster than it takes to write the word.

Why do you test your KWO?

If you can think of a complete sentence for each line of notes, you can use your notes to write a paper.

If you cannot make a complete sentence, you are not ready to write a paper. The KWO needs to be fixed.

Read	a line of notes.
Think	of a sentence.
Look up	so your eyes are not on the paper.
Speak	in complete sentences.

Adventures in Writing: Student Book

UNIT 2: WRITING FROM NOTES

New Style

Style

Just as there are many styles of clothes, there are many styles of language. Below are two sentences that say the same thing but with different styles.

> The tornado caused damage.

> The fast spinning tornado flattened buildings and threw cars in the air.

You probably like the second sentence better because it is more descriptive. Readers cannot see, hear, or feel what is in your mind. You must fill in the details with descriptive words. The IEW elements of style give you the tools you need to create strong images and feelings.

Dress-Ups

Dress-ups help you "dress up" your writing. The IEW dress-ups are descriptive words, phrases, or clauses that you add to a sentence. You will learn six dress-ups. To show you have added a dress-up to a sentence, you should underline it. You may use more than one of a specific type of dress-up in a paragraph, but only underline one of each type in each paragraph.

-ly Adverb Dress-Up

In this lesson you will learn the first dress-up: the -ly adverb.

An -ly adverb is an adverb that ends in -ly. Adverbs are words that modify verbs, adjectives, or other adverbs. Most often they tell *how* or *when* something is done.

Notice how the -ly adverbs change the meaning of this sentence:

> The tornado destroyed trees.
> The tornado <u>violently</u> destroyed trees.
> The tornado <u>suddenly</u> destroyed trees.

Now you choose an -ly adverb.

> The tornado _____ destroyed trees.

 From now on, include an -ly adverb in each paragraph you write. Mark the -ly adverb by underlining it.

-ly Adverb

Students benefit from looking at word lists. A longer list of -ly adverbs can be found on the *Portable Walls for Structure and Style® Students* as well as the IEW Writing Tools App.

From this point forward students should include one -ly adverb in each paragraph they write. Although more than one -ly adverb may be placed in a paragraph, only one should be underlined.

This dress-up now appears on the checklist.

Style Practice

-ly Adverb Dress-Up

You must include an -ly adverb in each paragraph you write. Use the list found in this lesson, on the *Portable Walls™ for Structure and Style® Students*, or on the IEW Writing Tools App.

What -ly adverbs could express . . .

1. how the tornado spins?

   violently, uncontrollably, powerfully

2. how the tornado forms?

   naturally, commonly, usually

3. when the tornado picks up dust and debris?

   abruptly, suddenly, instantly

4. how the tornado destroys buildings, trees, and bridges?

   devastatingly, forcefully, mercilessly

-ly Adverbs

abruptly
beneficially
boldy
bravely
cautiously
cleverly
commonly
dangerously
destructively
devastatingly
finally
fiercely
forcefully
furiously
gingerly
ingeniously
instantly
naturally
powerfully
safely
suddenly
usually
uncontrollably
violently
wildly

Suggested Answers

To model strong word choices, the suggested answers have come from a thesaurus.

Vocabulary

Students may use vocabulary words from any lesson if they desire. *Abruptly* and *forcefully* are vocabulary words.

UNIT 2: WRITING FROM NOTES

Vocabulary

The sample sentences are only suggestions. If students ask for help, offer an idea. Listen as they read their sentences aloud.

Vocabulary Practice

Listen   to someone read the vocabulary words for Lesson 5 aloud.

Speak   them aloud yourself.

Read   the definitions and sample sentences on the vocabulary cards.

Write   two sentences using one of this lesson's vocabulary words in each sentence. You may use derivatives of the words.

abruptly

Tornadoes pick up dust and debris abruptly.

forcefully

A tornado can forcefully toss a car in the air.

Think   about the words. Can you use them in your paragraph?

A vocabulary word that is an -ly adverb may count as an -ly adverb and a vocabulary word.

Lesson 5: Tornadoes

Unit 2 Composition Checklist
Lesson 5: Tornadoes

Writing from Notes

Name: _____

STRUCTURE
- ☐ name and date in upper left-hand corner _____ 5 pts
- ☐ composition double-spaced _____ 5 pts
- ☐ title centered _____ 10 pts
- ☐ checklist on top, final draft, rough draft, key word outline _____ 10 pts

STYLE
¶1 Dress-Ups (underline)
- ☐ -ly adverb _____ 10 pts

MECHANICS
- ☐ capitalization _____ 15 pts
- ☐ end marks and punctuation _____ 15 pts
- ☐ complete sentences _____ 15 pts
- ☐ correct spelling _____ 15 pts

VOCABULARY
- ☐ vocabulary words - label *(voc)* in left margin or after sentence

Total: _____ 100 pts

Custom Total: _____ pts

Motivate

Because positive reinforcement is a wonderful motivator, consider incorporating a ticket system as described on page 241. When you return graded papers, give a ticket for each vocabulary word used.

Checklist

The box under style indicates one paragraph. Students should include and mark one -ly adverb.

Although more than one -ly adverb may be placed in a paragraph, only one should be underlined.

UNIT 2: WRITING FROM NOTES

Intentionally blank so the checklist can be removed.

Lesson 6: Benjamin Franklin's Lightning Rod

Structure: Unit 2: Writing from Notes
                  title rule

Style: no new style

Subject: Benjamin Franklin's lightning rod

UNIT 2: WRITING FROM NOTES

Lesson 6: Benjamin Franklin's Lightning Rod

Goals

- to practice the Units 1 and 2 structural models
- to write a 1-paragraph summary
- to create a title
- to use new vocabulary words: *cautiously, cleverly*

Assignment Schedule

Day 1

1. Play Tic-Tac-Toe.
2. Read and discuss "Benjamin Franklin's Lightning Rod." Circle key words.
3. Write your KWO and then test it.

Day 2

1. Review your KWO from Day 1.
2. Read New Structure and complete Style Practice.
3. Begin writing your rough draft. Use your KWO.
4. Look at the checklist. Check each box as you complete each requirement.

Day 3

1. Look at the vocabulary cards for Lesson 6. Complete Vocabulary Practice.
2. Finish writing your rough draft. Use your KWO and the checklist. Follow the title rule to create a title.
3. Turn in your rough draft to your editor with the completed checklist attached.

Day 4

1. Review the vocabulary words and their meanings.
2. Write or type a final draft.
3. Paperclip the checklist, final draft, rough draft, and KWO together.

Tic-Tac-Toe

See Appendix IV for game directions. For this lesson use questions 1–7 and vocabulary words.

UNIT 2: WRITING FROM NOTES

Source Text

Benjamin Franklin's Lightning Rod

During a thunderstorm Benjamin Franklin flew a kite with a key attached to a special string. The kite had a thin rod at the top. When Franklin touched the key, he felt an electric shock. This experiment proved lightning was electricity. It led him to invent the lightning rod. A lightning rod is a thin metal rod attached to the top of a building. It guides the lightning to the ground so that the building does not burn.

Mechanics

The first time you write a name, write the first and last name. After the first time, write only the last name.

Sample Lesson 6: Benjamin Franklin's Lightning Rod

Key Word Outline

After you have circled two or three key words in each sentence, write your KWO. Use symbols, numbers, and abbreviations when possible.

I. _thunderstorm, BF, kite, 🔑, string_

1. _kite, rod, top_

2. _touched, 🔑, electric shock_

3. _experiment, lightning = electricity_

4. _→ invent, lightning rod_

5. _LR, metal, rod, ↑, building_

6. _guides, ⚡, ground, 🏠, X burn_

Test your KWO. First, write the pattern.

R _ead_ a line of notes.

T _hink_ of a sentence.

L _ook up_ so your eyes are not on the paper.

S _peak_ in complete sentences.

Source text titles are purposely vague. Students will create their own interesting or dramatic titles following the title rule.

UNIT 2: WRITING FROM NOTES

New Structure

Titles

An interesting title grabs a reader's attention. To create a title, repeat one to three key words from the final sentence.

This is the last sentence of "Tornadoes": The United States has more tornadoes than any other country.

Here are two possible titles:

> More Tornadoes
>
> Tornadoes in the United States

> "*Title repeats one to three key words from final sentence.*"

Title Capitalization

Capitalize the first word and the last word.

Capitalize all other words except
 articles (a, an, the),
 coordinating conjunctions (for, and, nor, but, or, yet, so),
 prepositions (such as in, over, on, without).

Practice

Since you have not yet written the final sentence of this assignment, create a title using one to three key words from the final sentence of the source text.

It guides the lightning to the ground so that the building does not burn.

Buildings No Longer Burn

From now on, make a title for your compositions by repeating one to three key words from the final sentence.

Titles

To form a title, key words in the last sentence sometimes need to be changed. That is fine. If students ask, offer suggestions.

Style Practice

-ly Adverb Dress-Up

You must include an -ly adverb in each paragraph you write. Use the list found on page 41, on the *Portable Walls for Structure and Style® Students*, or on the IEW Writing Tools App.

What -ly adverbs could express . . .

1. how Franklin touched the key?

   carefully, cautiously, gingerly

2. how Franklin invented the lightning rod?

   cleverly, ingeniously, intelligently

3. how the lightning rod guided lightning to the ground?

   beneficially, conveniently, safely

Look at your KWO and consider -ly adverbs to include in your paragraph.

UNIT 2: WRITING FROM NOTES

Vocabulary Practice

Listen   to someone read the vocabulary words for Lesson 6 aloud.

Speak   them aloud yourself.

Read   the definitions and sample sentences on the vocabulary cards.

Write   the part of speech and the definition beside the word.

cautiously

adverb; carefully avoiding danger or risk

cleverly

adverb; showing intelligent thinking

Think   about the words. Can you use them in your paragraph?

Lesson 6: Benjamin Franklin's Lightning Rod

Unit 2 Composition Checklist
Lesson 6: Benjamin Franklin's Lightning Rod

Writing from Notes

Name: _____

STRUCTURE
- ☐ name and date in upper left-hand corner _____ 5 pts
- ☐ composition double-spaced _____ 5 pts
- ☐ title centered and repeats 1–3 key words from final sentence _____ 10 pts
- ☐ checklist on top, final draft, rough draft, key word outline _____ 10 pts

STYLE
¶1 **Dress-Ups** (underline)
- ☐ -ly adverb _____ 10 pts

MECHANICS
- ☐ capitalization _____ 15 pts
- ☐ end marks and punctuation _____ 15 pts
- ☐ complete sentences _____ 15 pts
- ☐ correct spelling _____ 15 pts

VOCABULARY
- ☐ vocabulary words - label *(voc)* in left margin or after sentence

Total: _____ 100 pts
Custom Total: _____ pts

Checklist

The box under style indicates one paragraph. Students should include and mark one -ly adverb.

Adventures in Writing: Student Book

Intentionally blank so the checklist can be removed.

Lesson 7: Hannibal's War

Structure: Unit 2: Writing from Notes
Style: *who/which* clause
Subject: Hannibal's war

UNIT 2: WRITING FROM NOTES

Lesson 7: Hannibal's War

Goals

- to practice the Units 1 and 2 structural models
- to write a 1-paragraph summary
- to add a new dress-up: *who/which* clause
- to use new vocabulary words: *guide, terrified*

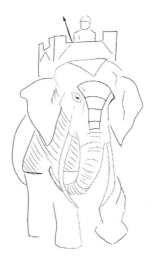

Assignment Schedule

Day 1

1. Play Elimination.
2. Read and discuss "Hannibal's War." Circle key words.
3. Write your KWO and then test it.

Day 2

1. Read New Style and complete Style Practice.
2. Review your KWO from Day 1.
3. Begin writing your rough draft. Use your KWO.
4. Look at the checklist. Check each box as you complete each requirement.

Day 3

1. Look at the vocabulary cards for Lesson 7. Complete Vocabulary Practice.
2. Finish writing your rough draft. Use your KWO and the checklist.
3. Turn in your rough draft to your editor with the completed checklist attached.

Day 4

1. Review the vocabulary words and their meanings.
2. Write or type a final draft.
3. Paperclip the checklist, final draft, rough draft, and KWO together.

Hannibal was a military general from Carthage. In 218 BC he tried to defeat the Romans by leading his army and war elephants across the treacherous mountains.

UNIT 2: WRITING FROM NOTES

Source Text

Hannibal's War

General Hannibal's enemies feared his war elephants. These beasts stood eleven feet tall, weighed six-thousand pounds, and wore armor. Trumpeting loudly, they trampled through enemy lines like tanks. They fought with their trunks and tusks. Hannibal took his war elephants across the Mediterranean Sea and over the Alps to surprise the Roman army. They would not expect him to arrive from the mountains. The Roman soldiers must have been frightened of Hannibal's war elephants.

Mechanics

Do not use contractions in academic writing.

Sample

Lesson 7: Hannibal's War

Key Word Outline

After you have circled two or three key words in each sentence, write your KWO. Use symbols, numbers, and abbreviations when possible.

I. _____ GH, enemies, feared, elephants _____

   1. _____ 11 ft, 6,000 lbs, wore, armor _____

   2. _____ trumpeting, trampled, enemy ∥ _____

   3. _____ fought, trunks, tusks _____

   4. _____ H, elephants, ↷, Mediterranean Sea, Alps _____

   5. _____ Romans, X expect, arrive, mts _____

   6. _____ R soldiers, frightened, elephants _____

Test your KWO. First, write the pattern.

   R _ead_____ a line of notes.

   T _hink_____ of a sentence.

   L _ook up____ so your eyes are not on the paper.

   S _peak_____ in complete sentences.

Who/Which Clause

At this level, teach students to place commas around all *who/which* clauses.

As students become more sophisticated in their writing, they will learn that they do not use commas with essential *who/which* clauses.

The soldiers who saw the elephants shook with fear.

Not all soldiers shook with fear. Only the soldiers who saw the elephants shook with fear. The *who* clause is essential to the sentence.

However, at this level require students to place commas around all *who/which* clauses.

UNIT 2: WRITING FROM NOTES

New Style

Who/Which Clause Dress-Up

In this lesson you will learn another dress-up: *who/which* clause.

A *who/which* clause is a group of words that describes the noun it follows.

> Hannibal, who crossed the Alps, surprised the Roman army.

> The elephants, which trumpeted loudly, fought with their trunks and tusks.

Notice:

1. A *who/which* clause begins with the word *who* or *which*.

   Use *who* to refer to people and *which* to refer to places and things.

   To indicate a *who/which* clause, underline *who* or *which*.

2. The *who/which* clause describes a noun—a person, place, thing, or idea.

   Hannibal, who crossed the Alps, surprised the Roman army.

   The *elephants*, which trumpeted loudly, fought with their trunks and tusks.

3. The *who/which* clause is added to a sentence that is already complete.

   If you remove the *who/which* clause, a sentence must remain.

   Hannibal, who crossed the Alps, *surprised the Roman army.*

   If you only insert the word *who* or *which*, you will not have a sentence.

   Hannibal, who crossed the Alps (incomplete sentence)

❜ Place commas around a *who/which* clause.

> The elephants, which trumpeted loudly, fought with their trunks and tusks.

✎ From now on, include a *who/which* clause in each paragraph you write. Mark the *who/which* clause by underlining the word *who* or *which*.

Lesson 7: Hannibal's War

Style Practice

Who/Which Clause Dress-Up

Combine the statements using the word *who* or *which*.
Add commas. Underline *who* or *which*.

1. The beasts wore armor. The beasts trampled through enemy lines.

   The beasts, <u>which</u> wore armor, trampled through enemy lines.

   The beasts, <u>which</u> trampled through enemy lines, wore armor.

2. The soldiers did not expect Hannibal to arrive. The soldiers were frightened.

   The soldiers, <u>who</u> were frightened, did not expect Hannibal to arrive.

   The soldiers, <u>who</u> did not expect Hannibal to arrive, were frightened.

-ly Adverb Dress-Up

You must include an -ly adverb in each paragraph you write.

What -ly adverbs could express . . .

1. how the elephants fought?

   ferociously, fiercely, viciously, wildly

2. how Hannibal led the elephants?

   boldly, bravely, courageously, fearlessly

   Look at your KWO and consider dress-ups to include in your paragraph.

> **Who/Which Clause**
>
> Read the sentences and orally fill in the blanks several times. When students understand the pattern of the *who/which* clause, direct them to write.

UNIT 2: WRITING FROM NOTES

Vocabulary Practice

Listen   to someone read the vocabulary words for Lesson 7 aloud.

Speak   them aloud yourself.

Read   the definitions and sample sentences on the vocabulary cards.

Write   the correct words in the blanks. You may use derivatives of the words.

Hannibal ____**guided**____ his elephants across the mountains.

The Romans were ____**terrified**____ of Hannibal's elephants.

Think   about the words. Can you use them in your paragraph?

Vocabulary

A derivative (form of) the vocabulary word *guide* is needed to complete the first sentence. Help students add suffixes in order to spell words correctly.

Lesson 7: Hannibal's War

Unit 2 Composition Checklist
Lesson 7: Hannibal's War

Writing from Notes

Name: _____

Institute for Excellence in Writing

STRUCTURE
- ☐ name and date in upper left-hand corner _____ 5 pts
- ☐ composition double-spaced _____ 5 pts
- ☐ title centered and repeats 1–3 key words from final sentence _____ 10 pts
- ☐ checklist on top, final draft, rough draft, key word outline _____ 10 pts

STYLE
¶1 Dress-Ups (underline one of each)
- ☐ -ly adverb _____ 10 pts
- ☐ *who/which* clause _____ 10 pts

MECHANICS
- ☐ capitalization _____ 10 pts
- ☐ end marks and punctuation _____ 10 pts
- ☐ complete sentences _____ 15 pts
- ☐ correct spelling _____ 15 pts

VOCABULARY
- ☐ vocabulary words - label *(voc)* in left margin or after sentence

Total: _____ 100 pts
Custom Total: _____ pts

Checklist

Remind students that they must format their final drafts by following the directions on page 33.

Students should include and mark an -ly adverb and a *who/which* clause in the paragraph.

Teachers are free to adjust a checklist by requiring only the stylistic techniques that have become easy, plus one new one. EZ+1

Intentionally blank so the checklist can be removed.

Lesson 8: The Fox and the Crow, Part 1

Preparation: *Teaching Writing: Structure and Style*
Watch the sections for Unit 3: Retelling Narrative Stories.
At IEW.com/twss-help reference the TWSS Viewing Guides.

Structure: Unit 3: Retelling Narrative Stories
Style: no new style
Subject: an Aesop fable

UNIT 3: RETELLING NARRATIVE STORIES

Lesson 8: The Fox and the Crow, Part 1

Goals
- to learn the Unit 3 Retelling Narrative Stories structural model
- to create a 3-paragraph KWO using the Story Sequence Chart
- to use new vocabulary words: *crave, sly*

Assignment Schedule

Day 1

1. Play Vocabulary Find the Card.
2. Read New Structure—Retelling Narrative Stories.
3. Read and discuss "The Fox and the Crow."

   Who are the main characters?
   What does the fox want?
   How does the story end?

Day 2

1. Reread the source text.
2. Write a KWO for the first paragraph by answering the Story Sequence Chart questions for characters and setting.

   You may answer the questions in any order.
   You may use more than one line to answer one question.
   You may answer two questions on one line.
   You do not have to answer every question.

3. Test the first part of your KWO. Read. Think. Look up. Speak.

Day 3

1. Look at the vocabulary cards for Lesson 8. Complete Vocabulary Practice.
2. Reread the source text.
3. Write a KWO for the second paragraph by answering the Story Sequence Chart questions for conflict or problem.
4. Test the first and second parts of the KWO. Read. Think. Look up. Speak.

Unit 3

In this new unit students begin by reading a story. No longer are key words taken from each sentence; rather, key words are now found in developing key ideas.

Key ideas are formed by answering questions related to the Story Sequence Chart. For example, you will ask, "Who are the characters?" Form key words from the answer.

The same outlining rules apply: two or three key words per line; symbols, numbers, and abbreviations are free.

Exemplar

The Exemplars file contains a student's completed assignment for Lessons 8 and 9. The Exemplar is for the teacher and not intended to be used by the student.

See the blue page for download instructions.

UNIT 3: RETELLING NARRATIVE STORIES

Day 4

1. Review the vocabulary words and their meanings.

2. Reread the source text.

3. Write a KWO for the third paragraph by answering the Story Sequence Chart questions for climax and resolution.

4. Use your KWO to give an oral report to a friend or family member. Read. Think. Look up. Speak. If applicable, be prepared to give an oral report in class.

Lesson 8: The Fox and the Crow, Part 1

New Structure

Retelling Narrative Stories

In Unit 3 you will focus on story writing. You will no longer find key words in each sentence. Instead, you will choose key words by asking questions about a story using the Story Sequence Chart.

The Story Sequence Chart has three Roman numerals because the assignments in Unit 3 are three paragraphs long. Each paragraph has a purpose. The first paragraph tells about the people or animals in the story and when and where they live. The second paragraph tells about the conflict or problem. The third paragraph begins with the climax and ends with the resolution.

Use the Story Sequence Chart to think about the story. After you read a story, ask the questions in each section in any order.

The Story Sequence Chart

I. Characters and Setting
Who is in the story?
What are they like?
When does it happen?
Where do they live/go?

II. Conflict or Problem
What do they need/want?
What do they think?
What do they say and do?

III. Climax and Resolution
How is the problem/need resolved?
What happens after?
What is learned?

Motivate

Help students learn the Story Sequence Chart. Begin by helping students memorize what each paragraph is about: characters and setting, conflict or problem, climax and resolution.

Adventures in Writing: Student Book

UNIT 3: RETELLING NARRATIVE STORIES

Source Text

The Fox and the Crow

One morning a plain black crow sat on a branch, holding a piece of cheese in her beak. Along came a fox, who smelled the cheese. The fox stood under the tree, greeted the crow, and told her that she was beautiful. The crow was very pleased at this, but she could not reply because her mouth was full of cheese. The fox praised her beautiful eyes and shiny feathers. The crow was even more pleased but said nothing. She just sat on her branch and swelled with pride. The fox told her he had heard about her lovely voice. He begged the crow to sing a few notes for him. This was too much for the crow. She opened her beak wide, cawed loudly, and dropped the cheese right into the mouth of the waiting fox. The clever fox ate the cheese. He told the crow that her song was ugly and she should not believe everything she hears. Laughing, he trotted off into the woods.

Key Word Outline

Now that you have read the story, use the Story Sequence Chart to think about the story. Begin with the characters and setting. As you answer a question, write two or three key words on the KWO.

Lesson 8: The Fox and the Crow, Part 1

Before completing the KWO, remind students that this is a new unit and that key words are found differently. Key words are no longer found by looking at each sentence. Key words are found by using the Story Sequence Chart to ask and answer questions. Not all of the questions on this page need to be answered. Within each section, questions may be asked in any order that helps the story flow.

The KWOs in the Teacher's Manual are only samples. Every class and each student will have unique outlines.

Sample

Lesson 8: The Fox and the Crow, Part 1

Key Word Outline—Story Sequence Chart

Characters and Setting

- Who is in the story?
- What are they like?
- When does it happen?
- Where do they live/go?

I. crow, plain, proud
  1. C, branch, cheese, beak
  2. fox, sly, hungry
  3. tree, forest, farmhouse
  (4.) morning, bright, crisp

I. Characters and Setting

In this paragraph answer questions about the fox and the crow. Students must make up details for the setting.

Conflict or Problem

- What do the characters need or want?
- What do the characters think, say, do?
- What happens before the climax?

II. fox, wanted, cheese
  1. trick, flatter, distract
  2. praised, beautiful 👀, feathers
  3. C, pleased, blushed, silent
  (4.)

II. Conflict or Problem

In this paragraph answer questions about what the fox wants: the cheese.

Climax and Resolution

- What is the climax?
- What happens as a result?
- What is learned? (message, moral)

III. fox, begged, C, sing
  1. cawed, opened, beak
  2. cheese, dropped, F, mouth
  3. ☺ gobbled, cheese
  (4.) ♪, ugly, X believe, hear

III. Climax and Resolution

In this paragraph begin with the climax, which is when the fox begs the crow to sing.

Adventures in Writing: Student Book

Each Roman numeral indicates a different paragraph. Encourage students to use the KWO to tell back the story in complete sentences. Model the process as needed.

UNIT 3: RETELLING NARRATIVE STORIES

Vocabulary Practice

Listen   to someone read the vocabulary words for Lesson 8 aloud.

Speak   them aloud yourself.

Read   the definitions and sample sentences on the vocabulary cards.

Write   the part of speech and the definition beside the word.

crave

verb; to desire strongly

sly

adjective; clever in a dishonest way

Think   about the words. Can you use them in your story?

Vocabulary

Ask students if *sly* is an -ly adverb.

It is not! -ly adverbs have -ly as a suffix. If you remove the -ly ending, a word remains.

Sly can be made into an -ly adverb by adding the suffix -ly: *slyly*.

Lesson 9: The Fox and the Crow, Part 2

Structure: Unit 3: Retelling Narrative Stories
Style: no new style
Subject: an Aesop fable

UNIT 3: RETELLING NARRATIVE STORIES

Lesson 9: The Fox and the Crow, Part 2

Goals
- to write a 3-paragraph story from the KWO
- to review vocabulary words

Assignment Schedule

Day 1
1. Play Vocabulary Lightning.
2. Review your KWO from Lesson 8.
3. Use your KWO. Write a rough draft for your first paragraph.
4. Look at the checklist. Check each box as you complete each requirement.

Day 2
1. Complete Style Practice.
2. Read what you wrote on Day 1.
3. Use your KWO. Write a rough draft for your second paragraph.
4. Look at the checklist. Check each box as you complete each requirement.

Day 3
1. Complete Vocabulary Review.
2. Read what you wrote on Days 1 and 2.
3. Use your KWO. Write a rough draft for your third paragraph.
4. Look at the checklist. Check each box as you complete each requirement.
5. Turn in your rough draft to your editor with the completed checklist attached.

Day 4
1. Study for Vocabulary Quiz 2. It will cover words from Lessons 5–8.
2. Write or type a final draft.
3. Paperclip the checklist, final draft, rough draft, and KWO together.

UNIT 3: RETELLING NARRATIVE STORIES

Style Practice
-ly Adverb Dress-Up

The best -ly adverbs are words that add meaning to your sentence by telling how or when something is done. Find a verb (an action word) and ask *how* or *when*.

Write a few ideas for an -ly adverb dress-up on the lines below each sentence. Choose your favorite to write on the blank in the sentence.

The crow __*sleepily*__ sat on a branch.

-ly adverbs __*peacefully, (sleepily,) normally*__

1. The crow __*firmly*__ held a piece of cheese in her beak.

   -ly adverbs __*tightly, firmly, gleefully*__

2. The fox __*deceivingly*__ told the crow she was beautiful.

   -ly adverbs __*cleverly, craftily, deceivingly*__

3. The fox __*triumphantly*__ gobbled the cheese.

   -ly adverbs __*immediately, triumphantly, hungrily*__

Look at your KWO and consider -ly adverbs to include in your story.

Who/Which Clause Dress-Up

A *who/which* clause describes the noun it follows. If a *who/which* clause is misplaced, the sentence does not make sense. Read the following sentences and decide where the *who/which* clause belongs. Rewrite the sentences correctly.

1. A crow sat on a branch, who held a piece of cheese.

   A crow, who held a piece of cheese, sat on a branch.

2. The fox stood under a tree, who told the crow she was beautiful.

   The fox, who told the crow she was beautiful, stood under a tree.

3. The fox told the crow that her song was ugly, who ate the cheese.

   The fox, who ate the cheese, told the crow her song was ugly.

Look at your KWO and consider *who/which* clauses to include in your story.

Who/Which Clause

When a *who/which* clause describes an animal that acts like a human, begin the *who/which* clause with *who*.

UNIT 3: RETELLING NARRATIVE STORIES

Vocabulary Review

Listen   to someone read the vocabulary words for Lessons 5–8 aloud.

Speak   them aloud yourself.

Read   the definitions and sample sentences on the vocabulary cards.

Write   the words that match the definitions.

terrified — extremely afraid

abruptly — very suddenly and unexpectedly

cleverly — showing intelligent thinking

crave — to desire strongly

forcefully — with great strength; powerfully

cautiously — carefully avoiding danger or risk

sly — clever in a dishonest way

guide — to lead in a certain path

Think   about the words and their meanings. Which vocabulary words could you use in your story?

cleverly, crave, abruptly, sly

Lesson 9: The Fox and the Crow, Part 2

Unit 3 Composition Checklist
Lesson 9: The Fox and the Crow

Retelling Narrative Stories

Name: _____

STRUCTURE
- ☐ name and date in upper left-hand corner _____ 5 pts
- ☐ composition double-spaced _____ 5 pts
- ☐ story follows Story Sequence Chart _____ 8 pts
- ☐ title centered and repeats 1–3 key words from final sentence _____ 8 pts
- ☐ each paragraph contains at least four sentences _____ 8 pts
- ☐ checklist on top, final draft, rough draft, key word outline _____ 8 pts

STYLE
¶1 ¶2 ¶3 **Dress-Ups** (underline one of each) (3 pts each)
- ☐ ☐ ☐ -ly adverb _____ 9 pts
- ☐ ☐ ☐ *who/which* clause _____ 9 pts

MECHANICS
- ☐ capitalization _____ 10 pts
- ☐ end marks and punctuation _____ 10 pts
- ☐ complete sentences _____ 10 pts
- ☐ correct spelling _____ 10 pts

VOCABULARY
- ☐ vocabulary words - label *(voc)* in left margin or after sentence

Total: _____ 100 pts

Custom Total: _____ pts

Checklist

The three boxes under style indicate three paragraphs. Students should include and mark an -ly adverb and a *who/which* clause in each paragraph.

Teachers are free to adjust a checklist by requiring only the stylistic techniques that have become easy, plus one new one. EZ+1

Adventures in Writing: Student Book

Intentionally blank so the checklist can be removed.

Lesson 10: The Theft of Thor's Hammer, Part 1

Structure: Unit 3: Retelling Narrative Stories
Style: no new style
Subject: a Norse myth

UNIT 3: RETELLING NARRATIVE STORIES

Lesson 10: The Theft of Thor's Hammer, Part 1

Goals

- to practice the Unit 3 structural model
- to create a 3-paragraph KWO using the Story Sequence Chart
- to take Vocabulary Quiz 2
- to use new vocabulary words: *desperately, vanish*

Assignment Schedule

Day 1

1. Take Vocabulary Quiz 2.
2. Read and discuss "The Theft of Thor's Hammer."

Day 2

1. Reread the source text.
2. Write a KWO for the first paragraph by answering the Story Sequence Chart questions for characters and setting. Ask the four questions in any order.
3. Test the first part of your KWO. Read. Think. Look up. Speak.

Day 3

1. Look at the vocabulary cards for Lesson 10. Complete Vocabulary Practice.
2. Reread the source text.
3. Write a KWO for the second paragraph by answering the Story Sequence Chart questions for conflict or problem.
4. Test the first and second parts of the KWO. Read. Think. Look up. Speak.

Day 4

1. Review the vocabulary words and their meanings.
2. Reread the source text.
3. Write a KWO for the third paragraph by answering the Story Sequence Chart questions for climax and resolution.
4. Test the KWO. Read. Think. Look up. Speak.

Adventures in Writing: Student Book

Source Text

The Theft of Thor's Hammer

Thor was the Norse god of thunder. He lived in Asgard, the home of the gods. He had a special hammer. When he threw it, the hammer came back to him. Thor used his hammer to defend Asgard against the giants. One morning Thor's hammer was gone. Thrym, the king of the giants, had stolen it. He said he would return it if the goddess Freya became his wife. Freya was the goddess of love.

Thor dressed in a wedding gown and wore Freya's golden necklace so that he looked like her. A veil hid his face. He hoped the disguise would fool Thrym. When Thor reached the palace for the wedding, the giant king welcomed his bride. The king placed the hammer on his bride's lap. Thor tore the veil from his face. The giants realized the bride was Thor! They tried to run away. Thor and his hammer were too powerful. Thor defeated the giants and returned to Asgard with his hammer.

On the left are the Story Sequence Chart questions that students ask about the story as they create the KWO. Use the helpful hints to guide students to answer the questions. Within each section, ask the questions in any order to help the story make sense.

Sample

Lesson 10: The Theft of Thor's Hammer, Part 1

Key Word Outline—Story Sequence Chart

Characters and Setting

I. Thor, Norse, g, thunder

1. Asgard, home, gods
2. special, hammer
3. threw, came, back
(4.) hammer, defend, giants

Who is in the story?
What are they like?
When does it happen?
Where do they live/go?

Conflict or Problem

II. Thor, hammer, gone

1. Thrym, 👑, giants, stole
2. return, Freya, wife
3. Thor, disguise, fool, 👑
(4.) gown, necklace, veil

What do the characters need or want?
What do the characters think, say, do?
What happens before the climax?

Climax and Resolution

III. king, welcomed, bride

1. hammer, bride's lap
2. X veil, giants, 👀 Thor
3. Thor + hammer = powerful
(4.) defeated, giants, → home

What is the climax?
What happens as a result?
What is learned? (message, moral)

I. Characters and Setting

In this paragraph answer questions about when and where the story takes place. Tell about Thor and his special hammer.

II. Conflict or Problem

In this paragraph answer questions about the main conflict: Thor's hammer was gone. Thrym will return it if Freya becomes his wife.

III. Climax and Resolution

In the final paragraph begin with the climax, which is when the king welcomed his bride.

Adventures in Writing: Student Book

UNIT 3: RETELLING NARRATIVE STORIES

Vocabulary Practice

Listen to someone read the vocabulary words for Lesson 10 aloud.

Speak them aloud yourself.

Read the definitions and sample sentences on the vocabulary cards.

Write two sentences using one of this lesson's vocabulary words in each sentence. You may use derivatives of the words.

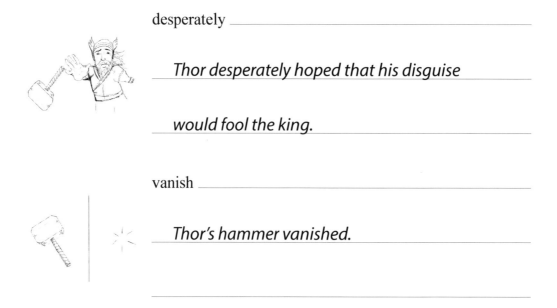

desperately

Thor desperately hoped that his disguise would fool the king.

vanish

Thor's hammer vanished.

Think about the words. Can you use them in your story?

Lesson 11: The Theft of Thor's Hammer, Part 2

Structure: Unit 3: Retelling Narrative Stories
Style: strong verb, banned words: *say/said*
Subject: a Norse myth

UNIT 3: RETELLING NARRATIVE STORIES

Lesson 11: The Theft of Thor's Hammer, Part 2

Goals

- to write a 3-paragraph story from the KWO
- to add a new dress-up: strong verb
- to ban weak verbs: *say/said*
- to use new vocabulary words: *deceive, declare*

Assignment Schedule

Day 1

1. Review your KWO from Lesson 10.
2. Use your KWO. Write a rough draft for your first paragraph.
3. Look at the checklist. Check each box as you complete each requirement.

Day 2

1. Read New Style and complete Style Practice.
2. Read what you wrote on Day 1.
3. Use your KWO. Write a rough draft for your second paragraph.
4. Look at the checklist. Check each box as you complete each requirement.

Day 3

1. Look at the vocabulary cards for Lesson 11. Complete Vocabulary Practice.
2. Read what you wrote on Days 1 and 2.
3. Use your KWO. Write a rough draft for your third paragraph.
4. Look at the checklist. Check each box as you complete each requirement.
5. Turn in your rough draft to your editor with the completed checklist attached.

Day 4

1. Tell someone the title rule. Do you know it word perfect?
2. Write or type a final draft.
3. Paperclip the checklist, final draft, rough draft, and KWO together.

Adventures in Writing: Student Book

> *Strong Verb*
>
> This is the third dress-up introduced in this book. This means three dress-ups now appear on the checklist, and three dress-ups should be underlined in each paragraph written for this lesson. The pace for adding stylistic techniques can be adjusted if a student needs time to practice previous dress-ups. Adjust the checklist if necessary.

UNIT 3: RETELLING NARRATIVE STORIES

New Style
Strong Verb Dress-Up

In this lesson you will learn another dress-up: strong verb.

Every verb has a subject.
To determine if a word is a verb, use the verb test.

I ___ .

It ___ .

Underline the verbs.

paper   escaped   student   laugh   find   swim

Every sentence has a verb, but not all verbs are strong verbs. Strong verbs show action. They help a reader imagine what someone or something is doing.

Banned Words

Boring verbs should be avoided. For this reason, you will not be allowed to use certain verbs in your writing assignments. These are *banned words*.

From now on, the verb *say/said* is banned.

Thrym *said* that he wanted to marry Freya.

What verbs are stronger than *said*? Notice how changing the verb changes what you imagine when you read the sentence. On the line below, add to the list of synonyms.

Synonyms for *say/said* __remarked, murmured__ *declared, bellowed, roared*

For help finding strong verbs, use a thesaurus or your vocabulary words. You can also look at the lists of substitutes on the *Portable Walls for Structure and Style Students* or the IEW Writing Tools App.

✏️ From now on, include a strong verb in each paragraph you write.
Mark the strong verb by underlining it.

⊘ BANNED WORDS   VERB: SAY/SAID

Lesson 11: The Theft of Thor's Hammer, Part 2

Style Practice

Who/Which Clause Dress-Up

Combine the statements using the word *who* or *which*.
Add commas. Underline *who* or *which*.

1. Thor lived in Asgard. Asgard was the home of the gods.

   Thor lived in Asgard, <u>which</u> was the home of the gods.

2. Thrym wanted to marry Freya. Freya was the goddess of love.

   Thrym wanted to marry Freya, <u>who</u> was the goddess of love.

3. Thor dressed in a wedding gown. He wore Freya's golden necklace.

   Thor, <u>who</u> dressed in a wedding gown, wore Freya's golden necklace.

   Thor, <u>who</u> wore Freya's golden necklace, dressed in a wedding gown.

   Look at your KWO and consider *who/which* clauses to include in your story.

Who/Which Clause

Read the sentences and orally fill in the blanks several times. When students understand the pattern of the *who/which* clause, direct them to write.

Dress-Ups

Encourage students to find nouns on the KWO and then think of actions the noun did. After students list strong verbs, have them look at an -ly adverb list for words that modify the verbs.

UNIT 3: RETELLING NARRATIVE STORIES

Strong Verb Dress-Up and -ly Adverb Dress-Up

List strong verbs and -ly adverbs to include in your story.

strong verbs *resembled, concealed, escaped, owned*

-ly adverbs *unfortunately, cleverly, easily, finally*

Vocabulary Practice

Listen to someone read the vocabulary words for Lesson 11 aloud.

Speak them aloud yourself.

Read the definitions and sample sentences on the vocabulary cards.

Write the correct words in the blanks. You may use derivatives of the words.

Thor's disguise ___*deceived*___ Thrym.

Thrym ___*declared*___ that he wanted to marry Freya.

Think about the words. Can you use them in your story?

A vocabulary word that is a strong verb may count as a strong verb and a vocabulary word.

Lesson 11: The Theft of Thor's Hammer, Part 2

Unit 3 Composition Checklist
Lesson 11: The Theft of Thor's Hammer

Retelling Narrative Stories

Name: _____

STRUCTURE
- ☐ name and date in upper left-hand corner _____ 2 pts
- ☐ composition double-spaced _____ 3 pts
- ☐ story follows Story Sequence Chart _____ 7 pts
- ☐ title centered and repeats 1–3 key words from final sentence _____ 7 pts
- ☐ each paragraph contains at least four sentences _____ 7 pts
- ☐ checklist on top, final draft, rough draft, key word outline _____ 7 pts

STYLE
¶1 ¶2 ¶3 **Dress-Ups** (underline one of each) (3 pts each)
- ☐ ☐ ☐ -ly adverb _____ 9 pts
- ☐ ☐ ☐ *who/which* clause _____ 9 pts
- ☐ ☐ ☐ strong verb _____ 9 pts

CHECK FOR BANNED WORDS (-1 pt for each use):
say/said _____ pts

MECHANICS
- ☐ capitalization _____ 10 pts
- ☐ end marks and punctuation _____ 10 pts
- ☐ complete sentences _____ 10 pts
- ☐ correct spelling _____ 10 pts

VOCABULARY
- ☐ vocabulary words - label *(voc)* in left margin or after sentence

Total: _____ 100 pts
Custom Total: _____ pts

Checklist

The three boxes under style indicate three paragraphs. Students should include and mark an -ly adverb, a *who/which* clause, and a strong verb in each paragraph.

Teachers are free to adjust a checklist by requiring only the stylistic techniques that have become easy, plus one new one. EZ+1

Intentionally blank so the checklist can be removed.

Lesson 12: Leif Eriksson

Preparation: *Teaching Writing: Structure and Style*
Watch the sections for Unit 4: Summarizing a Reference.
At IEW.com/twss-help reference the TWSS Viewing Guides.

Structure: Unit 4: Summarizing a Reference
topic-clincher sentences

Style: banned words: *see/saw*

Subject: Leif Eriksson

UNIT 4: SUMMARIZING A REFERENCE

Lesson 12: Leif Eriksson

Goals

- to learn the Unit 4 Summarizing a Reference structural model
- to learn and use the topic-clincher rule
- to create a KWO
- to ban weak verbs: *see/saw*
- to write a 1-paragraph report
- to use new vocabulary words: *abundantly, notice*

Assignment Schedule

Day 1

1. Play Around the World.
2. Read New Structure—Summarizing a Reference.
3. Memorize the topic-clincher rule.
4. Read and discuss "Leif Eriksson."
5. Your assignment is to write a paragraph about how Leif Eriksson discovered America. That is why *Eriksson, discovered, America* is on the Roman numeral line (the topic line) of the KWO.
6. Reread the source text and put marks by four or five facts that are most interesting or important. These are facts that support the topic.
7. Write the facts on the KWO.

Day 2

1. Test your KWO.
2. Say the topic-clincher rule.
3. Write a topic sentence.
4. Complete Structure Practice.
5. Begin writing your rough draft. Use your KWO.
6. Look at the checklist. Check each box as you complete each requirement.

Unit 4

In this new unit the KWO is formed by taking key words from interesting and important facts found in a source text. Initially, teachers will likely need to assist students as they limit their notes. Model the process. Let students choose facts they think are interesting or important, limiting them to 4–5 total facts.

In this unit students learn to organize writing by beginning each paragraph with a topic sentence and ending each paragraph with a clincher sentence.

Exemplar

The Exemplars file contains a student's completed assignment for Lesson 12. The Exemplar is for the teacher and not intended to be used by the student.

See the blue page for download instructions.

UNIT 4: SUMMARIZING A REFERENCE

Day 3

1. Look at the vocabulary cards for Lesson 12. Complete Vocabulary Practice.
2. Practice saying the topic-clincher rule.
3. Complete Style Practice.
4. Finish writing your rough draft. Use your KWO and the checklist.
5. Turn in your rough draft to your editor with the completed checklist attached.

Day 4

1. Review the vocabulary words and their meanings.
2. Write or type a final draft.
3. Practice saying the topic-clincher rule.
4. Highlight or bold the key words *Eriksson, discovered, America* in the topic and clincher sentences.
5. Paperclip the checklist, final draft, rough draft, and KWO together.

Read this page to introduce Unit 4: Summarizing a Reference. Talk about the difference between the compositions students wrote for Unit 3 and the compositions they will write for Unit 4. Read about the topic and clincher sentences and their purpose.

Lesson 12: Leif Eriksson

New Structure

Summarizing a Reference

In Unit 4 you will write reports by summarizing a reference. You will find information in source texts. These sources have more information than you need. You will not note every fact from the source text. Instead, choose four or five interesting or important facts and "*SOME*-a-rize."

When you write a report, organize facts into paragraphs. Each paragraph begins with a topic sentence, contains facts, and ends with a clincher sentence.

1 topic = 1 paragraph

Topic Sentence

> The topic sentence tells what the paragraph is about. It is the first sentence of the paragraph. When you write the KWO, ask "What will the paragraph be about?" The key words on the Roman numeral line state the topic.

Facts

> On the other lines of the KWO, write facts that support the topic. To find facts, read the source text and look for five to six things that you find interesting or important. To help you remember each fact that you choose, write two or three key words about the fact on the KWO. Use symbols, numbers, and abbreviations when possible.

Clincher Sentence

> The clincher sentence reminds the reader what the paragraph was about. It is the last sentence of the paragraph. The KWO ends with the word *clincher*. Do not place key words on the clincher line. Instead when you write your rough draft, repeat (same word) or reflect (synonym of the word) two or three key words from the topic line.

> " **The topic sentence and the clincher sentence MUST repeat or reflect two or three key words.** "

Motivate

Help students learn the topic-clincher rule. If teaching to a classroom of students, advise students to be ready to recite the rule in order to enter class next time.

Locate Key Words

Guide students to find 4–5 facts. Reread each sentence. Ask your students, "Is that interesting or important?" If they answer yes, place a check mark by the fact or sentence.

Allow students to choose facts that they find interesting or important. Very likely their facts will differ from the ones chosen in this Teacher's Manual.

UNIT 4: SUMMARIZING A REFERENCE

Source Text

Leif Eriksson

Leif Eriksson was a Viking explorer. He lived in Greenland. When he was sailing back to Greenland from Norway in 1000 AD, a storm blew his ship off course. After many days the ocean calmed, and he saw land. He sailed to the shore near a beautiful forest and rolling hills. Eriksson and his men liked the land and decided to stay several months. They built houses and enjoyed the fruits and vegetables that grew in the rich soil. Eriksson named the new land Vineland because many grapes grew there. He had landed in Newfoundland on the Canadian coast. Leif Eriksson is believed to be the first European to reach North America.

Institute for Excellence in Writing

Lesson 12: Leif Eriksson

Before completing the KWO, remind students that this is a new unit and that key words are found differently. The key words on the Roman numeral line state the topic. Lines 1–4 (5) are for key words from facts, not from each sentence. Ask which facts interest them. Help them limit the number of facts they choose. Do not put key words for a clincher on the KWO. Direct students to write the clincher sentence when they write the paragraph.

The KWOs in the Teacher's Manual are only samples. Every class and each student will have unique outlines.

Sample

Lesson 12: Leif Eriksson

Key Word Outline

You will write a paragraph about how Leif Eriksson discovered America. That is why *Eriksson, discovered, America* is on the Roman numeral line (the topic line) of the KWO.

Did you put marks by four or five facts that are most interesting or important? Some facts must be left out. You are *SOME-a-rizing*.

Write the facts on the KWO.

I. Topic: _Eriksson, discovered, America_

1. _1000 AD, Norway → G, storm, blew, ⛵_

2. _new, land, ☺, forest, ⌒⌒_

3. _++ grapes, named, Vineland_

4. _land = Newfoundland, CA coast_

(5.) _____

Clincher

Test your KWO. For the clincher, repeat or reflect the words on the topic line.

Topic Sentence

The topic sentence tells what the paragraph is about. Use the key words on the topic line (or synonyms of those words) to write a topic sentence.

Leif Eriksson *was a Viking explorer, who* **discovered America**.

Clincher

Discuss ideas for a clincher sentence using two or three key words that repeat or reflect words written on the topic sentence line.

Here is a sample clincher sentence:

Eriksson discovered America.

Adventures in Writing: Student Book

UNIT 4: SUMMARIZING A REFERENCE

Structure Practice
Sample Paragraph

The following paragraph is a short report about Erik the Red. Of course, there is too much information about this man to be placed in a single paragraph. Therefore, the author has chosen a specific topic about Erik the Red to write about.

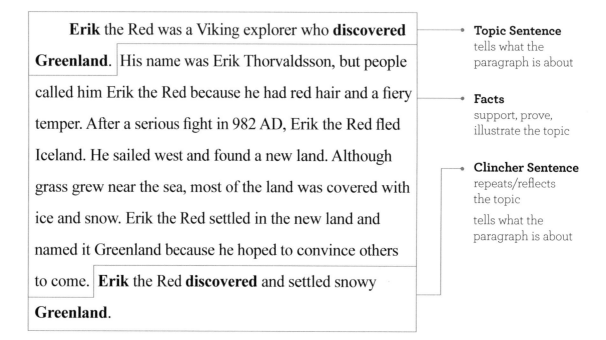

Topic Sentence
tells what the paragraph is about

Facts
support, prove, illustrate the topic

Clincher Sentence
repeats/reflects the topic
tells what the paragraph is about

1. Write the topic-clincher rule. _The topic sentence and the clincher sentence MUST repeat or reflect two or three key words._

2. In the sample paragraph, *Erik, discovered, Greenland* are bold. Where did these key words come from?

   the topic line of the key word outline

Lesson 12: Leif Eriksson

Style Practice

Strong Verb Dress-Up

The verb *say/said* is banned. In this lesson another verb is banned: *see/saw*. In each pair of sentences below, a verb is in italics. Underline the verb that is stronger.

1. From the ship they could *see* rolling hills.
   From the ship they could *detect* rolling hills.

2. Leif Eriksson *saw* land.
   Leif Eriksson *noticed* land.

To avoid these banned words, use a thesaurus or your vocabulary words or look at the lists of substitutes on the *Portable Walls for Structure and Style Students* or the IEW Writing Tools App.

Strong Verb Dress-Up and -ly Adverb Dress-Up

List strong verbs and -ly adverbs to include in your report.

strong verbs _spotted, noticed, resided, arrived_

-ly adverbs _violently, finally, abundantly, probably_

Who/Which Clause Dress-Up

Combine the statements using the word *who* or *which*.
Add commas. Underline *who* or *which*.

Eriksson and his men liked the land. The land had many vegetables.

Eriksson and his men liked the land, <u>which</u> had many vegetables.

Look at your KWO and consider dress-ups to include in your report.

⊘ BANNED WORDS   VERBS: SAY/SAID, SEE/SAW

UNIT 4: SUMMARIZING A REFERENCE

Vocabulary Practice

Listen   to someone read the vocabulary words for Lesson 12 aloud.

Speak   them aloud yourself.

Read   the definitions and sample sentences on the vocabulary cards.

Write   the part of speech and the definition beside the word.

   abundantly

adverb; richly supplied

   notice

verb; to become aware of

Think   about the words. Can you use them in your report?

Lesson 12: Leif Eriksson

Unit 4 Composition Checklist
Lesson 12: Leif Eriksson

Summarizing a Reference

Name: _____

Institute for Excellence in Writing

STRUCTURE
- ☐ name and date in upper left-hand corner _____ 2 pts
- ☐ composition double-spaced _____ 3 pts
- ☐ title centered and repeats 1–3 key words from final sentence _____ 10 pts
- ☐ topic-clincher sentences repeat or reflect 2–3 key words (highlight or bold) _____ 10 pts
- ☐ checklist on top, final draft, rough draft, key word outline _____ 5 pts

STYLE
¶1 Dress-Ups (underline one of each)
- ☐ -ly adverb _____ 10 pts
- ☐ *who/which* clause _____ 10 pts
- ☐ strong verb _____ 10 pts

CHECK FOR BANNED WORDS (-1 pt for each use):
say/said, see/saw _____ pts

MECHANICS
- ☐ capitalization _____ 10 pts
- ☐ end marks and punctuation _____ 10 pts
- ☐ complete sentences _____ 10 pts
- ☐ correct spelling _____ 10 pts

VOCABULARY
- ☐ vocabulary words - label *(voc)* in left margin or after sentence

Total: _____ 100 pts
Custom Total: _____ pts

Checklist

Notice that the checklist requires students to highlight or bold topic-clincher key words.

Dress-ups should continue to be underlined.

Teachers are free to adjust a checklist by requiring only the stylistic techniques that have become easy, plus one new one. EZ+1

Lesson 13: Hagia Sophia

Structure: Unit 4: Summarizing a Reference
Style: no new style
Subject: Hagia Sophia

UNIT 4: SUMMARIZING A REFERENCE

Lesson 13: Hagia Sophia

Goals

- to practice the Unit 4 structural model
- to write a 1-paragraph report
- to use new vocabulary words: *colossal, proudly*

Assignment Schedule

Day 1

1. Play a vocabulary game from the Teacher's Manual.
2. Review New Structure—Summarizing a Reference from Lesson 12.
3. Read and discuss "Hagia Sophia."
4. Your assignment is to write a paragraph about a cat that lived in Hagia Sophia. Write the key words for this topic *(Hagia Sophia, cat, special)* on the Roman numeral line (the topic line) of the KWO.
5. Reread the source text and write four or five facts on the KWO.

Day 2

1. Test your KWO and write a topic sentence.
2. Complete Style Practice.
3. Begin writing your rough draft. Use your KWO.
4. Look at the checklist. Check each box as you complete each requirement.

Day 3

1. Look at the vocabulary cards for Lesson 13. Complete Vocabulary Practice.
2. Finish writing your rough draft. Use your KWO and the checklist.
3. Turn in your rough draft to your editor with the completed checklist attached.

Day 4

1. Review the vocabulary words and their meanings.
2. Write or type a final draft. Highlight or bold the key words.
3. Paperclip the checklist, final draft, rough draft, and KWO together.

UNIT 4: SUMMARIZING A REFERENCE

Source Text

Hagia Sophia

The Hagia Sophia is a stunning building in Turkey that holds more than one surprise. It has a huge dome and marble pillars and was built almost 1,500 years ago. Recently, it was also the home to a gentle gray cat named Gli. Gli had green eyes that were a little bit crossed. She acted like a queen as she walked around the beautiful rooms. She loved to pose for pictures with people who visited the splendid building. Famous people like President Obama petted her when they visited. Gli lived in the Hagia Sophia for sixteen years. She died on June 11, 2020. She is buried in a special place in the Hagia Sophia garden.

Mechanics

When a date includes the month, day, and year, place a comma between the day and year. If the date is placed in the middle of a sentence, place a comma on both sides of the year.

Students must write key words on the topic line, the Roman numeral line. Since the assignment states what the paragraph must be about, the key words for the topic line must be *Hagia Sophia, cat, special*. The name *Hagia Sophia* is a proper noun and counts as one word on the KWO.

Sample Lesson 13: Hagia Sophia

Key Word Outline

You will write a paragraph about a cat that lived in Hagia Sophia. Write the key words for this topic *(Hagia Sophia, cat, special)* on the topic line.

Did you put marks by four or five facts that are most interesting or important? Some facts must be left out. You are *SOME-a-rizing*.

Write the facts on the KWO.

I. Topic: *Hagia Sophia, cat, special*

1. *Gli, gentle, green 👀*
2. *rooms, dome, 1500 yrs, Turkey*
3. *♡, posed, pictures*
4. *famous, petted, visited*
(5.) *16 yrs, died, 6/11/2020, buried, HS garden*

Clincher

Test your KWO. For the clincher, repeat or reflect the words on the topic line.

Topic Sentence

The topic sentence tells what the paragraph is about. Use the key words on the topic line (or synonyms of those words) to write a topic sentence.

*A **special cat** named Gli lived in **Hagia Sophia**.*

Writing the KWO

Students will likely need continued help. Model the process by writing a sample KWO on the whiteboard for them to see. Help students limit which interesting or important facts they choose.

Clincher

Discuss ideas for a clincher sentence using two to three key words that repeat or reflect words written on the topic sentence line.

Here is a sample clincher sentence:

Gli is remembered as the **special cat** that lived in **Hagia Sophia**.

Adventures in Writing: Student Book

UNIT 4: SUMMARIZING A REFERENCE

Style Practice
-ly Adverb Dress-Up

Not every -ly adverb works in every sentence. Consider the sample sentence and three options below.

Gli __*proudly*__ walked around the rooms.

    fearfully   slowly   (proudly)

Fearfully is not true. Gli felt comfortable in her home.
Slowly fits, but it implies she walked in a slow manner.
Proudly is best. Gli acted like a queen when she walked.

Two -ly adverbs are correct, but one is better than the other.

Read the following sentences and choose the best -ly adverb.

1. Gli's eyes were _____ crossed.

    tenderly   (slightly)   unfortunately

2. People _____ petted the cat.

    helplessly   mostly   (gently)

3. Gli _____ posed for pictures.

    (usually)   angrily   wildly

Look at your KWO and thoughtfully consider -ly adverbs that you can purposefully include in your report.

-ly Adverb

Tenderly does not work. *Unfortunately* is a weak choice because it does not give additional meaning to the sentence. *Slightly* is best.

Helplessly does not work. *Mostly* is a weak choice because it does not give additional meaning to the sentence. *Gently* is best.

Angrily does not work. *Wildly* is a weak choice. It is unlikely that she posed in a wild manner. *Usually* is best.

Strong Verb Dress-Up and -ly Adverb Dress-Up

On the first line below each sentence, write strong verbs that could replace the italicized banned verb. On the second line, write ideas for -ly adverbs that you could use with the strong verbs.

1. People *said* the cat's eyes were crossed.

   strong verbs *noted, remarked, stated*

   -ly adverbs *surprisingly, curiously, rudely*

2. Gli *saw* visitors every day.

   strong verbs *noticed, spied, observed*

   -ly adverbs *usually, commonly, excitedly*

Who/Which Clause Dress-Up

Add a *who/which* clause. Add commas. Underline *who* or *which*.

1. Gli *,who had green eyes,* loved posing for pictures.

2. The building *, which was built 1,500 years ago,* has a huge dome and marble pillars.

Look at your KWO and consider dress-ups to include in your report.

UNIT 4: SUMMARIZING A REFERENCE

Vocabulary Practice

Listen   to someone read the vocabulary words for Lesson 13 aloud.

Speak   them aloud yourself.

Read   the definitions and sample sentences on the vocabulary cards.

Write   two sentences using one of this lesson's vocabulary words in each sentence. You may use derivatives of the words.

colossal

The Hagia Sophia has a colossal dome.

proudly

Gli proudly walked around the rooms of the Hagia Sophia.

Think   about the words. Can you use them in your report?

Lesson 13: Hagia Sophia

Unit 4 Composition Checklist
Lesson 13: Hagia Sophia

Summarizing a Reference

Name: _____

STRUCTURE
- ☐ name and date in upper left-hand corner ___ 2 pts
- ☐ composition double-spaced ___ 3 pts
- ☐ title centered and repeats 1–3 key words from final sentence ___ 10 pts
- ☐ topic-clincher sentences repeat or reflect 2–3 key words (highlight or bold) ___ 10 pts
- ☐ checklist on top, final draft, rough draft, key word outline ___ 5 pts

STYLE
¶1 Dress-Ups (underline one of each)
- ☐ -ly adverb ___ 10 pts
- ☐ *who/which* clause ___ 10 pts
- ☐ strong verb ___ 10 pts

CHECK FOR BANNED WORDS (-1 pt for each use):
say/said, see/saw ___ pts

MECHANICS
- ☐ capitalization ___ 10 pts
- ☐ end marks and punctuation ___ 10 pts
- ☐ complete sentences ___ 10 pts
- ☐ correct spelling ___ 10 pts

VOCABULARY
- ☐ vocabulary words - label *(voc)* in left margin or after sentence

Total: ___ 100 pts
Custom Total: ___ pts

Motivate

If you are using the ticket system as described on page 241, give a ticket for each vocabulary word used when you return graded papers.

Checklist

Teachers are free to adjust a checklist by requiring only the stylistic techniques that have become easy, plus one new one. EZ+1

Lesson 14: John Muir

Structure: Unit 4: Summarizing a Reference
Style: banned words: *go/went*
Subject: John Muir

UNIT 4: SUMMARIZING A REFERENCE

Lesson 14: John Muir

Goals

- to practice the Unit 4 structural model
- to ban weak verbs: *go/went*
- to write a 1-paragraph report
- to review vocabulary words

Assignment Schedule

Day 1

1. Play the Question Game.
2. Read and discuss "John Muir."
3. Your assignment is to write a paragraph about John Muir's adventure. Write the key words on the Roman numeral line (the topic line) of the KWO.
4. Reread the source text and write four or five facts on the KWO.

Day 2

1. Test your KWO and write a topic sentence.
2. Complete Style Practice.
3. Begin writing your rough draft. Use your KWO.
4. Look at the checklist. Check each box as you complete each requirement.

Day 3

1. Complete Vocabulary Review.
2. Finish writing your rough draft. Use your KWO and the checklist.
3. Turn in your rough draft to your editor with the completed checklist attached.

Day 4

1. Study for Vocabulary Quiz 3. It will cover words from Lessons 10–13.
2. Write or type a final draft. Highlight or bold the key words.
3. Paperclip the checklist, final draft, rough draft, and KWO together.

Question Game

See Appendix IV for game directions. For this lesson use questions 1–10, 13–19, and vocabulary words.

Adventures in Writing: Student Book

Stickeen was a small terrier that belonged to John Muir's friend. The naturalist initially disliked the dog, considering it an overly coddled animal. After the perilous day among treacherous crevasses on Brady Glacier, Muir developed a fondness for the "brave little dog" and wrote the memoir *Stickeen: An Adventure with a Dog and a Glacier*.

UNIT 4: SUMMARIZING A REFERENCE

Source Text

John Muir

John Muir went to Glacier Bay, Alaska, three times. In 1880 Muir and his little dog Stickeen were almost trapped on a glacier. When Muir finished studying the glacier, he and Stickeen began walking toward camp. Suddenly, the sky grew dark, and freezing rain began to fall. Trudging in the darkness, they soon found themselves surrounded on three sides by deep open cracks in the ice. The cracks were so deep that Muir could not see the bottom. After wandering in the darkness, Muir found a narrow bridge made of snow. Muir walked across, but Stickeen was too afraid. Muir called to the dog. Slowly, Stickeen took one step and then another until he safely crossed the bridge. Muir wrote a popular book about his adventure, which brought many tourists to Glacier Bay.

Mechanics

Place a comma between a city and state. If the city and state are placed in the middle of a sentence, place a comma on both sides of the state.

Students must again write key words on the topic line, the Roman numeral line. Ask students what the paragraph must be about. (John Muir, adventure)

Guide students to place the key words *Muir, adventure* on the topic line. Ask students if they think the adventure was exciting or terrifying.

Sample

Lesson 14: John Muir

Key Word Outline

Next to the Roman numeral, write *Muir (subject)*, *adventure (topic)*. The third word should describe *adventure*. If you want to write about an exciting adventure, write *exciting*. If you want to write about a terrifying adventure, write *terrifying*.

Re-read the source text and write four or five facts to support the topic.

Write the facts on the KWO.

I. Topic: *Muir, adventure, exciting*

1. *1800, JM, Stickeen, trapped, Glacier Bay*
2. *dark, cracks, ice*
3. *wandering, narrow, bridge,* ☁
4. *JM, crossed, Stickeen, ++ afraid*
(5.) *JM, called, Stickeen, crossed*

Clincher

Test your KWO. For the clincher, repeat or reflect the words on the topic line.

Topic Sentence

The topic sentence tells what the paragraph is about. Use the key words on the topic line (or synonyms of those words) to write a topic sentence.

John Muir had an **exciting adventure** in Glacier Bay.

Topic

Remind students that the key words on the topic line state the topic of the paragraph.

Students use and bold these words when they write their topic and clincher sentences.

Clincher

Discuss ideas for a clincher sentence using two to three key words that repeat or reflect words written on the topic sentence line.

Here is a sample clincher sentence:

John Muir and his dog returned safely from their **exciting adventure** in Glacier Bay.

UNIT 4: SUMMARIZING A REFERENCE

Style Practice

Strong Verb Dress-Up

The verbs *say/said* and *see/saw* are banned. In this lesson another verb is banned: *go/went*. In each pair of sentences below, a verb is in italics. Underline the verb that is stronger.

1. John Muir decided to *go* to Glacier Bay.
   John Muir decided to *explore* Glacier Bay.

2. Stickeen *went* to the other side.
   Stickeen *crossed* to the other side.

To avoid these banned words, use a thesaurus or your vocabulary words or look at the lists of substitutes on the *Portable Walls for Structure and Style Students* or the IEW Writing Tools App.

On the line below, list synonyms for *go/went*.

Synonyms for *go/went* ____explored, traveled, journeyed____

-ly Adverb Dress-Up

Not every -ly adverb works in every sentence. Read the following sentences and choose the best -ly adverb.

1. John Muir _____ studied the glacier.

   loudly   (diligently)   certainly

2. He _____ hiked in Alaska with a dog by his side.

   (bravely)   happily   accidentally

   Look at your KWO and thoughtfully consider strong verbs and -ly adverbs that you can purposefully include in your report.

⊘ BANNED WORDS   VERBS: SAY/SAID, SEE/SAW, GO/WENT

-ly Adverb

Loudly does not work. *Certainly* is a weak choice because it does not give additional meaning to the sentence. *Diligently* is best.

Accidentally does not work. *Happily* is a weak choice. It is unlikely that he hiked in a happy manner. At times he may have been cold or discouraged. *Bravely* is best.

Lesson 14: John Muir

Strong Verb Dress-Up and -ly Adverb Dress-Up

List strong verbs and -ly adverbs to include in your report.

strong verbs ___hiked, detected, discovered___

-ly adverbs ___eagerly, unfortunately, finally___

Who/Which Clause Dress-Up

A *who/which* clause describes the noun it follows. If a *who/which* clause is misplaced, the sentence does not make sense. Read the following sentences and decide where the *who/which* clause belongs. Rewrite the sentences correctly.

1. John Muir crossed the bridge, <u>who</u> called to the dog.

   John Muir, <u>who</u> called to the dog, crossed the bridge.

2. The bridge allowed them to cross to safety, <u>which</u> was narrow.

   The bridge, <u>which</u> was narrow, allowed them to cross to safety.

Look at your KWO and consider dress-ups to include in your report.

Dress-Ups

Encourage students to find nouns on the KWO and then think of actions the noun did. After students list strong verbs, have them look at an -ly adverb list for words that modify the verbs.

Who/Which Clause

A *who/which* clause describes the noun it follows.

The first sentence states that the bridge called to the dog. That does not make sense. The *who* clause must follow the noun *John Muir*.

The second sentence states that safety was narrow. That does not make sense. The *which* clause must follow the noun *bridge*.

UNIT 4: SUMMARIZING A REFERENCE

Vocabulary Review

Listen   to someone read the vocabulary words for Lessons 10–13 aloud.

Speak   them aloud yourself.

Read   the definitions and sample sentences on the vocabulary cards.

Write   the words that match the definitions.

Word	Definition
deceive	to make someone believe something that is not true
colossal	great in size; huge
notice	to become aware of
desperately	showing an urgent need or desire
proudly	with pleasure or satisfaction from doing something
vanish	to disappear
abundantly	richly supplied
declare	to state in a strong and confident way

Think   about the words and their meanings. Which vocabulary words could you use in your report?

colossal, notice, desperately, vanish

Lesson 14: John Muir

Unit 4 Composition Checklist
Lesson 14: John Muir

Summarizing a Reference

Name: _____

STRUCTURE
- ☐ name and date in upper left-hand corner _____ 2 pts
- ☐ composition double-spaced _____ 3 pts
- ☐ title centered and repeats 1–3 key words from final sentence _____ 10 pts
- ☐ topic-clincher sentences repeat or reflect 2–3 key words (highlight or bold) _____ 10 pts
- ☐ checklist on top, final draft, rough draft, key word outline _____ 5 pts

STYLE
¶1 Dress-Ups (underline one of each)
- ☐ -ly adverb _____ 10 pts
- ☐ *who/which* clause _____ 10 pts
- ☐ strong verb _____ 10 pts

CHECK FOR BANNED WORDS (-1 pt for each use):
say/said, see/saw, go/went _____ pts

MECHANICS
- ☐ capitalization _____ 10 pts
- ☐ end marks and punctuation _____ 10 pts
- ☐ complete sentences _____ 10 pts
- ☐ correct spelling _____ 10 pts

VOCABULARY
- ☐ vocabulary words - label *(voc)* in left margin or after sentence

Total: _____ 100 pts
Custom Total: _____ pts

Checklist

Point out all the banned words on the checklist. Each of these words must be avoided when writing.

Teachers are free to adjust a checklist by requiring only the stylistic techniques that have become easy, plus one new one. EZ+1

Intentionally blank so the checklist can be removed.

Lesson 15: Magnets

Structure: Unit 4: Summarizing a Reference
Style: *because* clause
Subject: magnets

UNIT 4: SUMMARIZING A REFERENCE

Lesson 15: Magnets

Goals

- to practice the Unit 4 structural model
- to write a 2-paragraph report
- to add a new dress-up: *because* clause
- to take Vocabulary Quiz 3
- to use new vocabulary words: *effortlessly, metallic*

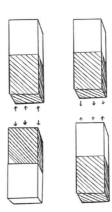

Assignment Schedule

Day 1

1. Play Build-a-Man.
2. Take Vocabulary Quiz 3.
3. Read New Structure—Identifying the Topic.
4. Read and discuss "Magnets" and complete Structure Practice.
5. Reread the source text and put marks by four or five interesting or important facts related to the first topic.
6. Write the facts on the KWO for the first paragraph.

Day 2

1. Reread the source text and put marks by four or five interesting or important facts related to the second topic.
2. Write the facts on the KWO for the second paragraph.
3. Read New Style and complete Style Practice.
4. Begin writing your rough draft. Use your KWO.
5. Look at the checklist. Check each box as you complete each requirement.

Day 3

1. Look at the vocabulary cards for Lesson 15. Complete Vocabulary Practice.
2. Finish writing your rough draft. Use your KWO and the checklist.
3. Turn in your rough draft to your editor with the completed checklist attached.

Unit 4

In this lesson students write two paragraphs about one subject. Both paragraphs will be about magnets. However, the topic of each paragraph will be different.

First, students divide the subject *magnets* into two topics: description and maglev train.

Second, students read the source text and find 4 or 5 interesting or important facts that are relevant to each topic.

Build-a-Man

See Appendix IV for game directions. For this lesson use the following phrases and bonus questions.

BANNED WORDS Bonus: What are the banned verbs? *say/said, see/saw, go/went*

TOPIC SENTENCE Bonus: What does the topic sentence do? *The topic sentence tells what the paragraph is about.*

UNIT 4: SUMMARIZING A REFERENCE

Day 4

1. Write or type a final draft. Highlight or bold the key words.
2. Paperclip the checklist, final draft, rough draft, and KWO together.

New Structure

Identifying the Topic

Subject

> The subject is the thing you research—the thing you write about. A subject of a paper may be a person, place, event, animal, or issue.

Topic

> The topic is the division of the thing you research—a thing within the subject.
>
> > If the subject is house, the possible topics (divisions) may be kitchen, bedroom, layout, history, location, owners, etc.
> >
> > If the subject is cats, the possible topics (divisions) may be characteristics, senses, behavior, lifespan, breeds, play, domestication, etc.

if **1 topic = 1 paragraph**

then **2 topics = 2 paragraphs**

Topic Line

> The topic line and topic sentence tell what the paragraph is about. When writing compositions with two or more paragraphs, follow the pattern: *subject, topic,* one more word *about the topic.*
>
> > If you write a paper about your house, the first paragraph might be about the kitchen. The key words on the KWO topic line could be *house, kitchen, busy.* The KWO facts and the sentences in the paragraph are about the busy kitchen in your house.
> >
> > The second paragraph might be about the bedroom. The key words on the KWO topic line could be *house, bedroom, cozy.* The KWO facts and the sentences in the paragraph are about the cozy bedroom in your house.

The three key words you place on the topic line determine the facts that you search for during the research process.

Subjects and Topics

Practice dividing subjects into topics.

Ask students what are possible topics (divisions) of the subject *moon*.

Possible topics include phases, characteristics, exploration, stories, eclipses.

Ask students what are possible topics (divisions) of the subject *horse*.

Possible topics include description, characteristics, wild, domestic, literature, history, movies, breeds, diseases.

Source Text

Magnets

A magnet is a piece of metal that can pull another piece of metal toward it. Each end of a magnet is called a pole. Magnets have a north pole and a south pole. The magnetic force between the two poles creates a magnetic field. Depending on how the poles are placed, the magnetic field will either pull objects together or push them apart. Most magnets are made from materials that contain iron. Materials such as cloth, paper, and wood do not work because they are weakly magnetic. Some of the fastest trains on the planet are powered by magnets. Magnetic levitation or maglev trains are high speed trains. They use the push and pull forces of magnets to move. When two north poles or two south poles are next to each other, the magnets will push away from each other. Maglev trains hover over guideways instead of running on wheels and tracks. Magnets with the same poles on the underside of the train and on the guideway lift the train off the guideway. Once the train is raised, the pulling force of magnets moves it forward. The pulling force of magnets is created when the north pole of one magnet is across from the south pole of another magnet. Instead of having an engine, a maglev train uses magnets with opposite poles on the sides of the train and guideway to pull it along the guideway. Trains with wheels are slowed down by the friction of the wheels on the tracks. Friction happens when two objects rub against each other and slow forward motion. Since maglev trains are traveling through air, there is very little friction. Therefore, maglev trains can reach speeds of several hundred miles per hour.

Structure Practice
Identifying the Topic
Now that you have read the source text, fill in these blanks.

1. The subject for this lesson is ___*magnets*___

2. Topics include ___*description, maglev train*___

3. On the KWO indicate the topics on the topic lines following this pattern: *subject*, *topic*, one more word *about the topic*.

Subjects and Topics

The subject is *magnets*.

The topics are *description* and *maglev train*, which are the divisions of the subject *magnets*. If necessary, tell students what to write in the blanks.

One more word *about the topic* is a descriptive word that narrows the topic. At this level, students can write any adjective that describes the topic.

A report is about one subject. Each paragraph is about a topic related to that subject.

Both paragraphs will be about the subject *magnets*. The topic of the first paragraph is *description*. Help students add an adjective to the topic line that describes *description*. The topic of the second paragraph is *maglev train*. Help students add an adjective to the topic line that describes *maglev train*.

Sample

Lesson 15: Magnets

Key Word Outline

Next to the first Roman numeral, write *magnets (subject), description (topic),* ___ (add one more word *about the topic*). Re-read the source text and write four or five facts to support the first topic.

Next to the second Roman numeral, write *magnets (subject), maglev train (topic),* ___ (add one more word *about the topic*). Re-read the source text and write four or five facts to support the second topic.

I. Topic: **magnets, description, interesting**
   1. metal + metal, pull
   2. N + S poles, magnetic force
   3. M, field, pull, push
   4. material, iron, X wood
   (5.) NP, across, SP = pulling force
   Clincher

Test your KWO. For the clincher, repeat or reflect the words on the topic line.

II. Topic: **magnets, maglev train, fast**
   1. X engine, high speed
   2. push + pull, magnets
   3. hover, guideways, X tracks
   4. N + N, under, lift, hovers
   (5.) N + S, sides, pull, guideway, > 100 mph
   Clincher

Test your KWO. For the clincher, repeat or reflect the words on the topic line.

Writing the KWO

Guide students to look for 4–5 interesting or important facts that support the chosen topic and to ignore the other facts. Supporting facts can be found in any portion of the source text.

Four dress-ups now appear on the checklist, and four dress-ups should be underlined in each paragraph written for this lesson. The pace for adding stylistic techniques can be adjusted if a student needs time to practice previous dress-ups. Adjust the checklist if necessary.

Because Clause

The *because* clause gives writers the chance to reason about cause and effect.

At this level, teach students to place the *because* clause after a sentence that is already complete.

As students become more sophisticated in their writing, they will learn that a *because* clause is an adverb clause and has two comma rules.

Use a comma after an adverb clause that comes before a main clause.

AC, MC

Do not use a comma before an adverb clause.

MC AC

At this level, tell students to place the *because* clause after a sentence that is already complete. No comma is needed.

UNIT 4: SUMMARIZING A REFERENCE

New Style

Because Clause Dress-Up

In this lesson you will learn another new dress-up: *because* clause.

A *because* clause is a group of words that begins with *because* and contains a subject and a verb. A *because* clause tells why.

because + subject + verb

A magnetic field is useful <u>because</u> it moves objects.

Maglev trains travel fast <u>because</u> they hover in the air.

Notice:

1. A *because* clause begins with the word *because*.

   To indicate a *because* clause, underline *because*.

2. A *because* clause contains a subject and a verb.

   A magnetic field is useful <u>because</u> *it moves* objects.

   Maglev trains travel fast <u>because</u> *they hover* in the air.

3. A *because* clause is added to a sentence that is already complete.

   A magnetic field is useful <u>because</u> it moves objects.

   Maglev trains travel fast <u>because</u> they hover in the air.

 Do not use a comma before a *because* clause.

Maglev trains travel fast <u>because</u> they hover in the air.

From now on, include a *because* clause in each paragraph you write. Mark the *because* clause by underlining the word *because*.

Institute for Excellence in Writing

Style Practice

Because Clause Dress-Up

Add a *because* clause to both sentences. Notice that the word *because* is underlined.

1. Objects push apart <u>because</u> *the same poles are next to each other.*

2. The maglev train moves forward <u>because</u> *magnets pull them along the guideway.*

Who/Which Clause Dress-Up

Add a *who/which* clause. Add commas. Underline *who* or *which*.

Maglev trains use magnets *, which pull or push them forward.*

Strong Verb Dress-Up and -ly Adverb Dress-Up

On the first line below the sentence, write strong verbs that could replace the italicized banned verb. On the second line, write ideas for -ly adverbs that you could use with the strong verbs.

The maglev train *went*.

strong verbs   *zoomed, floated, sped*

-ly adverbs   *effortlessly, silently, swiftly*

Look at your KWO and consider dress-ups to include in your report.

Because Clause

Read the main clause. Point out that it is a complete sentence.

Read the main clause again and ask, "Why?"

Orally fill in the blank several times with various answers.

When students understand the pattern of the *because* clause, direct them to write.

UNIT 4: SUMMARIZING A REFERENCE

Vocabulary Practice

Listen to someone read the vocabulary words for Lesson 15 aloud.

Speak them aloud yourself.

Read the definitions and sample sentences on the vocabulary cards.

Write two sentences using one of this lesson's vocabulary words in each sentence. You may use derivatives of the words.

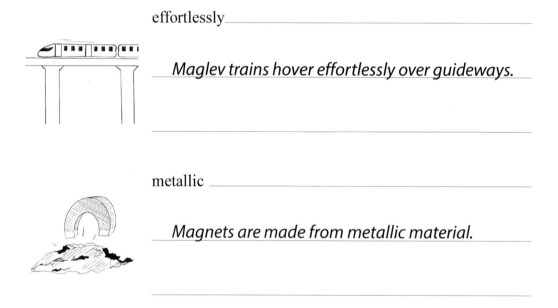

effortlessly

Maglev trains hover effortlessly over guideways.

metallic

Magnets are made from metallic material.

Think about the words. Can you use them in your report?

Lesson 15: Magnets

Unit 4 Composition Checklist
Lesson 15: Magnets

Summarizing a Reference

Name: _____

STRUCTURE

☐ name and date in upper left-hand corner _____ 2 pts
☐ composition double-spaced _____ 3 pts
☐ title centered and repeats 1–3 key words from final sentence _____ 8 pts
☐ topic-clincher sentences repeat or reflect 2–3 key words (highlight or bold) _____ 10 pts
☐ checklist on top, final draft, rough draft, key word outline _____ 5 pts

STYLE

¶1 ¶2 **Dress-Ups** (underline one of each) (4 pts each)
☐ ☐ -ly adverb _____ 8 pts
☐ ☐ *who/which* clause _____ 8 pts
☐ ☐ strong verb _____ 8 pts
☐ ☐ *because* clause _____ 8 pts

CHECK FOR BANNED WORDS (-1 pt for each use):
say/said, see/saw, go/went _____ pts

MECHANICS

☐ capitalization _____ 10 pts
☐ end marks and punctuation _____ 10 pts
☐ complete sentences _____ 10 pts
☐ correct spelling _____ 10 pts

VOCABULARY

☐ vocabulary words - label *(voc)* in left margin or after sentence

Total: _____ 100 pts
Custom Total: _____ pts

Checklist

Teachers are free to adjust a checklist by requiring only the stylistic techniques that have become easy, plus one new one. EZ+1

Intentionally blank so the checklist can be removed.

Lesson 16: Dolphins

Structure: Unit 4: Summarizing a Reference
Style: no new style
Subject: dolphins

UNIT 4: SUMMARIZING A REFERENCE

Lesson 16: Dolphins

Goals

- to practice the Unit 4 structural model
- to write a 2-paragraph report
- to use new vocabulary words: *mottled, tussle*

Assignment Schedule

Day 1

1. Read and discuss "Dolphins."
2. Complete Structure Practice.
3. Reread the source text and put marks by four or five interesting or important facts related to the first topic.
4. Write the facts on the KWO for the first paragraph.

Day 2

1. Reread the source text and put marks by four or five interesting or important facts related to the second topic.
2. Write the facts on the KWO for the second paragraph.
3. Complete Style Practice.
4. Begin writing your rough draft. Use your KWO.
5. Look at the checklist. Check each box as you complete each requirement.

Day 3

1. Look at the vocabulary cards for Lesson 16. Complete Vocabulary Practice.
2. Finish writing your rough draft. Use your KWO and the checklist.
3. Turn in your rough draft to your editor with the completed checklist attached.

Day 4

1. Write or type a final draft. Highlight or bold the key words.
2. Paperclip the checklist, final draft, rough draft, and KWO together.

Adventures in Writing: Student Book

Risso's dolphin (Grampus griseus) was named after the French naturalist Antoine Risso. The species name Risso's dolphin (plural Risso's dolphins) is correctly written with a capital letter and an apostrophe *s*.

UNIT 4: SUMMARIZING A REFERENCE

Source Text

Dolphins

Many types of dolphins swim in the world's oceans. Two common dolphins are Risso's and bottlenose dolphins. Risso's dolphins have round, blunt heads and are mottled. This means that they have gray and white patches. Bottlenose dolphins have short, thick snouts and mouths that look like large smiles. Other dolphins do not have this happy grin on their faces. Bottlenose dolphins are gray. Risso's dolphins are more scarred than other dolphins. They become scarred from playing and tussling with each other and from bites caused by squid and octopi, which they eat.

Dolphins must come out of the water for air because they are mammals. The longer that a dolphin can stay underwater the deeper it can dive. Since Risso's dolphins can stay underwater for almost thirty minutes, they can dive nearly one thousand feet below the surface. On the other hand, bottlenose dolphins can stay underwater for only twelve minutes, so they cannot dive that deep. A deep dive for a bottlenose dolphin is 150 feet.

Dolphins have been known to help people. Fishermen tell about dolphins guiding them to schools of fish. Swimmers have told stories about being lost and following dolphins back to shore. The most famous Risso's dolphin was Pelorus Jack. For twenty-four years, Jack guided ships through a dangerous part of Cook Strait, New Zealand. He appeared when ships entered a channel with reefs that could sink ships. Jack guided many ships to safety. Bottlenose dolphins also help people. Todd Endris was surfing when a great white shark attacked him. A group of bottlenose dolphins saved Endris by making a circle around him and allowing him to swim to shore. Dolphins are very smart.

Structure Practice
Identifying the Topic

Now that you have read the source text, fill in these blanks.

1. The subject for this lesson is _____dolphins_____

2. Topics include _____Risso's, bottlenose_____

3. On the KWO indicate the topics on the topic lines following this pattern: *subject*, *topic*, one more word *about the topic*.

Subjects and Topics

The subject is *dolphins*.

The topics are *Risso's* and *bottlenose*, which are the divisions of the subject *dolphins*. If necessary, tell students what to write in the blanks.

One more word *about the topic* is a descriptive word that narrows the topic. At this level, students can write any adjective that describes the topic.

A report is about one subject. Each paragraph is about a topic related to that subject.

Both paragraphs will be about the subject *dolphins*. The topic of the first paragraph is *Risso's*. Help students add an adjective to the topic line that describes *Risso's*. The topic of the second paragraph is *bottlenose*. Help students add an adjective to the topic line that describes *bottlenose*.

Writing the KWO

Guide students to look for 4–5 interesting or important facts that support the chosen topic and to ignore the other facts. Students are not limited to using facts found in a specific paragraph.

UNIT 4: SUMMARIZING A REFERENCE

Sample

Key Word Outline

Next to the first Roman numeral, write *dolphins (subject)*, *Risso's (topic)*, ____ (add one more word *about the topic*). Re-read the source text and write four or five facts to support the first topic.

Next to the second Roman numeral, write *dolphins (subject)*, *bottlenose (topic)*, ____ (add one more word *about the topic*). Re-read the source text and write four or five facts to support the second topic.

I. Topic: _____ *dolphins, Risso's, unique*
   1. _____ *blunt, head, mottled*
   2. _____ *tussle, bites, ++ scars*
   3. _____ *underwater, 30 min, 1000 ft*
   4. _____ *Pelorus Jack, 24 yrs, guided, ships*
   (5.) _____ *channel, dangerous, reefs, NZ*

   Clincher

Test your KWO. For the clincher, repeat or reflect the words on the topic line.

II. Topic: _____ *dolphin, bottlenose, fascinating*
   1. _____ *short, snout, smile*
   2. _____ *underwater, 12 min, dive, 150 ft*
   3. _____ *help, people*
   4. _____ *Todd Entries, surfing, shark*
   (5.) _____ *circle, swim, shore*

   Clincher

Test your KWO. For the clincher, repeat or reflect the words on the topic line.

Lesson 16: Dolphins

Style Practice

Who/Which Clause Dress-Up

Add a *who/which* clause. Add commas. Underline *who* or *which*.

1. The Risso's dolphin <u>, which can stay underwater for thirty minutes,</u> can dive one thousand feet.

2. Bottlenose dolphins <u>, which circled around Todd Entries,</u> helped him swim to shore.

Because Clause Dress-Up

Add a *because* clause. Underline the word *because*.

1. Risso's dolphins become scarred <u>because</u> they tussle with each other.

2. Bottlenose dolphins cannot dive deep <u>because</u> they can stay underwater for only twelve minutes.

   Look at your KWO and consider clauses to include in your report.

UNIT 4: SUMMARIZING A REFERENCE

Vocabulary Practice

Listen   to someone read the vocabulary words for Lesson 16 aloud.

Speak   them aloud yourself.

Read   the definitions and sample sentences on the vocabulary cards.

Write   the correct words in the blanks. You may use derivatives of the words.

The Risso's dolphin has gray and white ____*mottled*____ coloring.

When Risso's dolphins ____*tussle*____ with each other, they become scarred.

Think   about the words. Can you use them in your report?

Lesson 16: Dolphins

Unit 4 Composition Checklist
Lesson 16: Dolphins

Summarizing a Reference

Name: _____

STRUCTURE

- ☐ name and date in upper left-hand corner _____ 2 pts
- ☐ composition double-spaced _____ 3 pts
- ☐ title centered and repeats 1–3 key words from final sentence _____ 8 pts
- ☐ topic-clincher sentences repeat or reflect 2–3 key words (highlight or bold) _____ 10 pts
- ☐ checklist on top, final draft, rough draft, key word outline _____ 5 pts

STYLE

¶1 ¶2 **Dress-Ups** (underline one of each) (4 pts each)

- ☐ ☐ -ly adverb _____ 8 pts
- ☐ ☐ *who/which* clause _____ 8 pts
- ☐ ☐ strong verb _____ 8 pts
- ☐ ☐ *because* clause _____ 8 pts

CHECK FOR BANNED WORDS (-1 pt for each use):
say/said, see/saw, go/went _____ pts

MECHANICS

- ☐ capitalization _____ 10 pts
- ☐ end marks and punctuation _____ 10 pts
- ☐ complete sentences _____ 10 pts
- ☐ correct spelling _____ 10 pts

VOCABULARY

- ☐ vocabulary words - label *(voc)* in left margin or after sentence

Total: _____ 100 pts

Custom Total: _____ pts

Checklist

Teachers are free to adjust a checklist by requiring only the stylistic techniques that have become easy, plus one new one. EZ+1

UNIT 4: SUMMARIZING A REFERENCE

Intentionally blank so the checklist can be removed.

Lesson 17: Rooster, Part 1

Preparation: *Teaching Writing: Structure and Style*
Watch the sections for Unit 5: Writing from Pictures.
At IEW.com/twss-help reference the TWSS Viewing Guides.

Structure: Unit 5: Writing from Pictures
Style: no new style
Subject: a series of pictures about a rooster

UNIT 5: WRITING FROM PICTURES

Lesson 17: Rooster, Part 1

Goals

- to learn the Unit 5 Writing from Pictures structural model
- to create a KWO from a series of two pictures
- to learn to ask questions to get ideas for writing
- to use new vocabulary words: *commotion, slumber*

Assignment Schedule

Day 1

1. Play Tic-Tac-Toe.
2. Read New Structure—Writing from Pictures.
3. Look at the first picture in this lesson.
4. What do you see in the picture? Write the names of three things you see in the picture on the central fact line: the top line of the KWO.
5. Complete the KWO by asking yourself questions about the picture.
6. Test the KWO.

Day 2

1. Reread New Structure—Writing from Pictures.
2. Look at the second picture in this lesson.
3. What do you see in the picture? Write the names of three things you see in the picture on the central fact line: the top line of the KWO.
4. Complete the KWO by asking yourself questions about the picture.
5. Test the KWO.

Day 3

1. Look at the vocabulary cards for Lesson 17. Complete Vocabulary Practice.
2. Try to add at least one vocabulary word to your KWO.
3. Using your KWO, practice giving an oral report.

Unit 5

In this new unit the KWO is formed by looking at a series of pictures and asking good questions related to the pictures. The key words are formed from the answers to the questions.

This unit is not storytelling but rather event description. Help students form the topic sentence by focusing on the central fact of each picture. Develop the outline by asking questions to describe the event.

Tic-Tac-Toe

See Appendix IV for game directions. For this lesson use questions 1–19 and vocabulary words.

Exemplar

The Exemplars file contains a student's completed assignment for Lessons 17 and 18. The Exemplar is for the teacher and not intended to be used by the student.

See the blue page for download instructions.

UNIT 5: WRITING FROM PICTURES

Day 4

1. Review the vocabulary words and their meanings.

2. Use your KWO to give an oral report to a friend or family member. Read. Think. Look up. Speak. If applicable, be prepared to give an oral report in class.

New Structure

Writing from Pictures

In Unit 5 you will write paragraphs from a series of pictures. Although it may seem as if you are telling a story, your task is to describe each event.

Each paragraph begins with a central fact, contains details, and ends with a clincher sentence.

if **1 topic = 1 paragraph**

then **2 topics = 2 paragraphs**

and **3 topics = 3 paragraphs**

Central Fact
  The central fact tells what you see in the picture. It is the topic sentence of the paragraph. Think of this sentence as the caption that describes the picture. When you begin the KWO, ask yourself "What do I see in the picture?" As you answer, write three key words on the Roman numeral line.

Details
  On the other lines of the KWO, explain what is happening and how it came to be that way. Where do you find out what is happening? Ask yourself questions.

who?	where?	doing?	before?
what?	why?	thinking?	after?
when?	how?	feeling?	outside?
		saying?	

The answers to your questions become the details for the outline. As you answer a question, place two or three key words on the KWO. Use symbols, numbers, and abbreviations when possible.

Clincher Sentence
  The clincher sentence reminds the reader what you see in the picture. Because it is the clincher sentence, it must repeat or reflect two or three key words placed on the central fact line. What rule does that remind you of?

> **The topic sentence and the clincher sentence MUST repeat or reflect two or three key words.**

130 UNIT 5: WRITING FROM PICTURES

Look at both pictures and discuss how they relate to each other.

Writing the KWO

Ask students what they see in this picture. The picture on this page is of a crowing rooster standing on a building beside a house.

Tell students to write two or three things they see in the picture on the central fact line. Stick with the facts, the things you see.

Ask questions about the picture to determine what to place for notes on the rest of the KWO.

Although the central fact lines will be similar, every class and each student will have unique outlines.

UNIT 5: WRITING FROM PICTURES

Source

Rooster

I.

Key Word Outline   *Sample*   ?

I.   Central fact: _rooster, crowed, house_   who?
     1. _dawn, sun, rising_   what?
                                                               when?
     2. _neighborhood, quiet, Saturday_   where?
     3. _cats, dogs, ++ animals, Zzzz_   why?
                                                               how?
     4. _house, people, slumber_   doing?
     (5.) _rooster, woke, 1st, ☀_   thinking?
                                                               feeling?
Clincher repeats or reflects 2–3 key words of central fact.   saying?
                                                               before?
Test your KWO. Read. Think. Look up. Speak.   after?
    As you speak, the first sentence and the last sentence must describe
    the picture. Include words that tell what you see in the picture.   outside?

Institute for Excellence in Writing

Source

Rooster

II.

Key Word Outline

Sample

II. Central fact: _rooster, dog, man_   who?

1. _👤, tired, worked, late_   what?

    when?

2. _X work, sleep, late_   where?

3. _annoyed, yelled, "quiet!"_   why?

    how?

4. _neighbors, X sleep_   doing?

(5.) _++ loud, noise → laughter_   thinking?

    feeling?

Clincher repeats or reflects 2–3 key words of central fact.   saying?

    before?

Test your KWO. Read. Think. Look up. Speak.   after?
     As you speak, the first sentence and the last sentence must describe
the picture. Include words that tell what you see in the picture.   outside?

Writing the KWO

Ask students what they see in this picture. The picture on this page includes the rooster crowing, the dog howling, and the man yelling.

Tell students to write two or three things they see in the picture on the central fact line. Stick with the facts, the things you see.

Ask questions about the picture to determine what to place for notes on the rest of the KWO.

Although the central fact lines will be similar, every class and each student will have unique outlines.

A student might imagine the rooster is sounding an alarm because a wolf has come out of the woods nearby.

Another student might imagine the rooster is sounding an alarm because there is a burglar in the house while the family is away on vacation.

UNIT 5: WRITING FROM PICTURES

Vocabulary Practice

Listen to someone read the vocabulary words for Lesson 17 aloud.

Speak them aloud yourself.

Read the definitions and sample sentences on the vocabulary cards.

Write the part of speech and the definition beside the word.

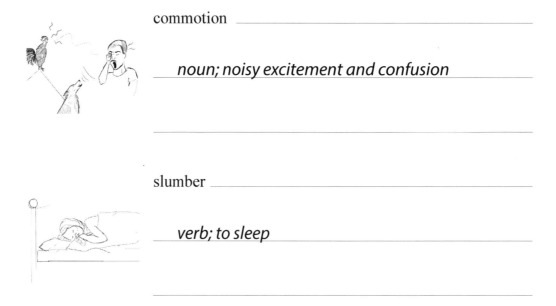

commotion

noun; noisy excitement and confusion

slumber

verb; to sleep

Think about the words. Can you use them in your composition?

Lesson 18: Rooster, Part 2

Structure: Unit 5: Writing from Pictures
Style: no new style
Subject: a series of pictures about a rooster

UNIT 5: WRITING FROM PICTURES

Lesson 18: Rooster, Part 2

Goals

- to write a 2-paragraph composition from the KWO
- to use new vocabulary words: *din, peacefully*

Assignment Schedule

Day 1

1. Play Elimination.
2. Review your KWO from Lesson 17.
3. Complete Structure Practice and write a rough draft for your first paragraph.
4. Make sure the clincher sentence repeats or reflects two or three key words of the central fact of the picture.
5. Look at the checklist. Check each box as you complete each requirement.

Day 2

1. Complete Style Practice.
2. Write a rough draft for your second paragraph. Use your KWO and the checklist.
3. Make sure the clincher sentence repeats or reflects two or three key words of the central fact of the picture.

Day 3

1. Look at the vocabulary cards for Lesson 18. Complete Vocabulary Practice.
2. Review your rough draft and look for places to add vocabulary or improve style.
3. Turn in your rough draft to your editor with the completed checklist attached.

Day 4

1. Review the vocabulary words and their meanings.
2. Write or type a final draft. Highlight or bold the key words.
3. Paperclip the checklist, final draft, rough draft, and KWO together.

Unit 5

In this lesson students use the KWO created in Lesson 17 to write a 2-paragraph composition.

Both paragraphs will begin with the central fact, a topic sentence which describes the picture. The clincher also describes the picture. The words that students bold indicate things the students see in the picture.

A topic sentence tells the reader what the rest of the paragraph is about. In Unit 5 the topic is the picture. To write the topic sentence of the paragraph, students write a sentence that contains the two or three words they placed on the topic line of the KWO. Following the topic-clincher rule, the clincher sentence also uses those same two or three words or synonyms of them. The topic sentence and the clincher sentence become captions for the picture.

Structure Practice

Topic Sentence

Use the words on the central fact line to write your topic sentence. If you wrote *rooster, crowed, house* on the central fact line, your topic sentence could be

A **rooster crowed** in front of a **house**.

Use the key words that you wrote on the first central fact (the topic line) to write a sentence that tells what you see in the picture. Highlight or bold the key words.

Answers will vary.

Continue your composition by forming sentences from the key words placed on the KWO. When you reach the clincher line, write a sentence that repeats or reflects two or three key words of the central fact. The clincher for the sample above might be

The **rooster** continued **crowing**, waking everyone in the **house**.

Style Practice

Who/Which Clause Dress-Up

Add a *who/which* clause to each sentence. Add commas. Underline *who* or *which*.

1. The rooster , <u>which</u> stood on the dog house, began to crow loudly.

2. The man , <u>who</u> had been asleep in the house, yelled at the rooster to stop crowing.

Strong Verb Dress-Up and -ly Adverb Dress-Up

On the first line below each sentence, write strong verbs that could replace the italicized banned verb. On the second line, write ideas for -ly adverbs that you could use with the strong verbs.

1. The man *said* that he could not sleep.

    strong verbs ____*yelled, hollered, screamed, complained*____

    -ly adverbs ____*angrily, furiously, sleepily, miserably*____

2. The man *saw* the animals.

    strong verbs ____*spied, eyed, stared, noticed*____

    -ly adverbs ____*continually, crossly, anxiously, amusingly*____

Because Clause Dress-Up

Add a *because* clause. Underline the word *because*.

1. The dog howled <u>because</u> *the rooster was making noise.*

2. The man opened the window <u>because</u> *he wanted the rooster to hear him.*

Look at your KWO and consider dress-ups to include in your composition.

UNIT 5: WRITING FROM PICTURES

Vocabulary Practice

Listen   to someone read the vocabulary words for Lesson 18 aloud.

Speak   them aloud yourself.

Read   the definitions and sample sentences on the vocabulary cards.

Write   two sentences using one of this lesson's vocabulary words in each sentence. You may use derivatives of the words.

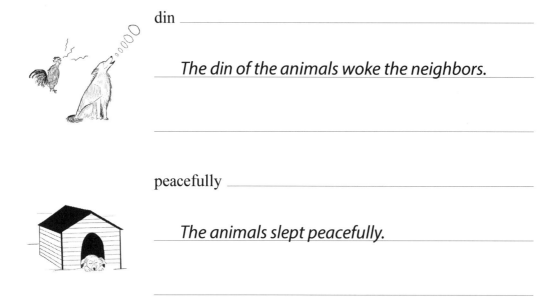

din _____

The din of the animals woke the neighbors.

peacefully _____

The animals slept peacefully.

Think   about the words. Can you use them in your composition?

Lesson 18: Rooster, Part 2

Unit 5 Composition Checklist
Lesson 18: Rooster

Writing from Pictures

Name: _____

STRUCTURE
- ☐ name and date in upper left-hand corner — 2 pts
- ☐ composition double-spaced — 3 pts
- ☐ title centered and repeats 1–3 key words from final sentence — 8 pts
- ☐ clincher sentences repeat or reflect 2–3 key words of central fact (highlight or bold) — 10 pts
- ☐ checklist on top, final draft, rough draft, key word outline — 5 pts

STYLE
¶1 ¶2 **Dress-Ups** (underline one of each) (4 pts each)
- ☐ ☐ -ly adverb — 8 pts
- ☐ ☐ *who/which* clause — 8 pts
- ☐ ☐ strong verb — 8 pts
- ☐ ☐ *because* clause — 8 pts

CHECK FOR BANNED WORDS (-1 pt for each use):
say/said, see/saw, go/went — ____ pts

MECHANICS
- ☐ capitalization — 10 pts
- ☐ end marks and punctuation — 10 pts
- ☐ complete sentences — 10 pts
- ☐ correct spelling — 10 pts

VOCABULARY
- ☐ vocabulary words - label *(voc)* in left margin or after sentence

Total: _____ 100 pts
Custom Total: _____ pts

Reminder

This is a 2-paragraph composition. If students add conversation, do not make them indent if the speaker changes.

Checklist

Teachers are free to adjust a checklist by requiring only the stylistic techniques that have become easy, plus one new one. EZ+1

Adventures in Writing: Student Book

Intentionally blank so the checklist can be removed.

Lesson 19: Treasure Map, Part 1

Structure: Unit 5: Writing from Pictures
Style: no new style
Subject: a series of pictures about two people and a treasure map

UNIT 5: WRITING FROM PICTURES

Lesson 19: Treasure Map, Part 1

Goals

- to practice the Unit 5 structural model
- to create a KWO from a series of three pictures
- to review vocabulary words

Assignment Schedule

Day 1

1. Play Vocabulary Pictionary or Vocabulary Lightning.
2. Review New Structure—Writing from Pictures from Lesson 17.
3. Write the KWO for the first picture.
4. Test the KWO.

Day 2

1. Write the KWO for the second picture.
2. Test the KWO.

Day 3

1. Complete Vocabulary Review.
2. Write the KWO for the third picture.
3. Test the KWO.
4. Using your KWO, practice giving an oral report.

Day 4

1. Study for Vocabulary Quiz 4. It will cover words from Lessons 15–18.
2. Use your KWO to give an oral report to a friend or family member. Read. Think. Look up. Speak. If applicable, be prepared to give an oral report in class.

Adventures in Writing: Student Book

Look at the series of pictures. The first picture is of hands holding a treasure map. The second picture shows two people looking at a treasure map outside. The third picture shows two people digging up rosebushes.

Source

Treasure Map

I.

II.

III.

Sample

Lesson 19: Treasure Map, Part 1

Key Word Outline

I. Central fact: _held, map, X_
   1. _Ethan, Nate, ? do_
   2. _afternoon, finished, chores_
   3. _decided, explore, attic_
   4. _found, old, box_
   (5.) _opened, map, treasure?_

   Clincher repeats or reflects 2–3 key words of central fact.

II. Central fact: _E+N, read, map, yard_
   1. _excited, pirate, hats_
   2. _wondered, ? neighbor's yard!_
   3. _ran, outside, back_
   4. _tree, creek, rosebush_ ✓
   (5.) _____

   Clincher repeats or reflects 2–3 key words of central fact.

III. Central fact: _shovels, dug, rosebush_
   1. _shed, shovels, rich!_
   2. _dug, all, rosebushes_
   3. _neighbor, 👀, 😟, stop!_
   4. _++ holes, hit, metal_
   (5.) _chest, gold, neighbor, 🙂_

   Clincher repeats or reflects 2–3 key words of central fact.

?

who?
what?
when?
where?
why?
how?
doing?
thinking?
feeling?
saying?
before?
after?
outside?

Writing the KWO

Students should write what they see in the picture on the central fact line. Stick with the facts, the things you see.

Guide students to ask questions to determine what to place for notes on the rest of the KWO.

Although the central fact lines will be similar, every class and each student will have unique outlines.

UNIT 5: WRITING FROM PICTURES

Vocabulary Review

Listen to someone read the vocabulary words for Lessons 15–18 aloud.
Speak them aloud yourself.
Read   the definitions and sample sentences on the vocabulary cards.
Write   the words that match the definitions.

Word	Definition
commotion	noisy excitement and confusion
slumber	to sleep
peacefully	calmly or quietly; without noise or excitement
din	a loud, confusing noise
tussle	to fight or struggle roughly
metallic	made of or containing metal
mottled	marked with colored spots or areas
effortlessly	easily

Think about the words and their meanings. Which vocabulary words could you use in your composition?

effortlessly, proudly, metallic

Lesson 20: Treasure Map, Part 2

Structure:	Unit 5: Writing from Pictures
Style:	quality adjective, banned words: *good, bad*
Subject:	a series of pictures about two people and a treasure map

UNIT 5: WRITING FROM PICTURES

Lesson 20: Treasure Map, Part 2

Goals

- to write a 3-paragraph composition from the KWO
- to add a new dress-up: quality adjective
- to ban weak adjectives: *good, bad*
- to take Vocabulary Quiz 4
- to use new vocabulary words: *delicate, discover*

Assignment Schedule

Day 1

1. Take Vocabulary Quiz 4.
2. Complete Structure Practice.
3. Use your KWO. Write a rough draft for your first paragraph.
4. Make sure the clincher sentence repeats or reflects two or three key words of the central fact of the picture.

Day 2

1. Read New Style and complete Style Practice.
2. Read what you wrote on Day 1.
3. Use your KWO. Write a rough draft for your second paragraph.
4. Make sure the clincher sentence repeats or reflects two or three key words of the central fact of the picture.

Day 3

1. Look at the vocabulary cards for Lesson 20. Complete Vocabulary Practice.
2. Use your KWO. Write a rough draft for your third paragraph.
3. Look at the checklist. Check each box as you complete each requirement.
4. Make sure the clincher sentence repeats or reflects two or three key words of the central fact of the picture.
5. Turn in your rough draft to your editor with the completed checklist attached.

UNIT 5: WRITING FROM PICTURES

Day 4

1. Review the vocabulary words and their meanings.

2. Write or type a final draft. Highlight or bold the key words.

3. Paperclip the checklist, final draft, rough draft, and KWO together.

Structure Practice

Topic Sentence

Use the words on the central fact line to write your topic sentence. If you wrote *held, map, X* on the central fact line, your topic sentence could be

The boys **held** the **map** with an **X**.

Use the key words that you wrote on the first central fact (the topic line) to write a sentence that tells what you see in the picture. Highlight or bold the key words.

Answers will vary.

Continue your composition by forming sentences from the key words placed on the KWO. When you reach the clincher line, write a sentence that repeats or reflects two or three key words of the central fact. The clincher for the sample above might be

The boys looked carefully at the **X** on the **map** they **held**.

New Style

Quality Adjective Dress-Up

In this lesson you will learn another dress-up: quality adjective.

An adjective describes a noun or pronoun.
It tells which one, what kind, how many, or whose.
To determine if a word is an adjective, use the adjective test.   **the ___ pen**

> *Quality Adjective*
>
> Encourage students to rapidly give many adjectives to describe the pen or person.
>
> *red, fat, fancy, old, new, broken, delightful, silly, terrible,* etc.
>
> For the rest of this course, one quality adjective should be underlined in every paragraph of the students' compositions.

Underline six adjectives.

horse	<u>sunny</u>	<u>nasty</u>	<u>famous</u>	wagon
dig	<u>delicious</u>	<u>sour</u>	<u>funny</u>	window

Banned Words

Boring adjectives like boring verbs should be avoided in writing. For this reason, you will not be allowed to use certain adjectives in your writing assignments.

From now on, the adjectives *good* and *bad* are banned.

> *Good* and *bad* are not very descriptive. They are ordinary. Quality adjectives like *kind* and *naughty* provide a strong image and feeling. What other quality adjectives are more descriptive than *good* and *bad*? On the lines below, add to the list of synonyms.

Synonyms for *good* __kind, helpful___   *excellent, splendid, prized*

Synonyms for *bad* __naughty, awful___   *unfortunate, horrible, terrible*

For help finding quality adjectives, use a thesaurus or your vocabulary words. Dropping the -ly from the words on the -ly adverb list will transform them into adjectives. You can also look at the lists of substitutes on the *Portable Walls for Structure and Style Students* or the IEW Writing Tools App.

 From now on, include a quality adjective in each paragraph you write.
Mark the quality adjective by underlining it.

⊘ BANNED WORDS   VERBS: SAY/SAID, SEE/SAW, GO/WENT   ADJECTIVES: GOOD, BAD

UNIT 5: WRITING FROM PICTURES

Dress-Ups

Encourage students to find nouns on the KWO and then think of actions the noun did. After students list strong verbs, have them look at an -ly adverb list for words that modify the verbs.

Style Practice
Strong Verb Dress-Up and -ly Adverb Dress-Up
List strong verbs and -ly adverbs to include in your composition.

strong verbs ____*Answers will vary.*____

-ly adverbs _____

Look at your KWO and consider dress-ups to include in your composition.

Vocabulary Practice

Listen to someone read the vocabulary words for Lesson 20 aloud.
Speak them aloud yourself.
Read the definitions and sample sentences on the vocabulary cards.
Write the correct words in the blanks. You may use derivatives of the words.

The boys __*discovered*__ an old map in the attic.

They dug up the __*delicate*__ rosebushes.

Think about the words. Can you use them in your composition?

A vocabulary word that is a quality adjective may count as a quality adjective and a vocabulary word.

Institute for Excellence in Writing

Lesson 20: Treasure Map, Part 2

Unit 5 Composition Checklist
Lesson 20: Treasure Map

Writing from Pictures

Name: _____

STRUCTURE

- ☐ name and date in upper left-hand corner _____ 2 pts
- ☐ composition double-spaced _____ 2 pts
- ☐ title centered and repeats 1–3 key words from final sentence _____ 3 pts
- ☐ clincher sentences repeat or reflect 2–3 key words of central fact (highlight or bold) _____ 6 pts
- ☐ checklist on top, final draft, rough draft, key word outline _____ 2 pts

STYLE

¶1 ¶2 ¶3 **Dress-Ups** (underline one of each) (3 pts each)

- ☐ ☐ ☐ -ly adverb _____ 9 pts
- ☐ ☐ ☐ *who/which* clause _____ 9 pts
- ☐ ☐ ☐ strong verb _____ 9 pts
- ☐ ☐ ☐ *because* clause _____ 9 pts
- ☐ ☐ ☐ quality adjective _____ 9 pts

CHECK FOR BANNED WORDS (-1 pt for each use):
say/said, see/saw, go/went, good, bad _____ pts

MECHANICS

- ☐ capitalization _____ 10 pts
- ☐ end marks and punctuation _____ 10 pts
- ☐ complete sentences _____ 10 pts
- ☐ correct spelling _____ 10 pts

VOCABULARY

- ☐ vocabulary words - label *(voc)* in left margin or after sentence

Total: _____ 100 pts
Custom Total: _____ pts

Adventures in Writing: Student Book

Reminder

This is a 3-paragraph composition. If students add conversation, do not make them indent if the speaker changes.

Checklist

Teachers are free to adjust a checklist by requiring only the stylistic techniques that have become easy, plus one new one. EZ+1

UNIT 5: WRITING FROM PICTURES

Intentionally blank so the checklist can be removed.

Lesson 21: Roanoke, Part 1

Preparation: *Teaching Writing: Structure and Style*
Watch the sections for Unit 6: Summarizing Multiple References.
At IEW.com/twss-help reference the TWSS Viewing Guides.

Structure: Unit 6: Summarizing Multiple References
Style: no new style
Subject: the Roanoke people

UNIT 6: SUMMARIZING MULTIPLE REFERENCES

Lesson 21: Roanoke, Part 1

Goals

- to learn the Unit 6 Summarizing Multiple References structural model
- to create source outlines from multiple references
- to create a fused outline
- to use new vocabulary words: *skilled, weir*

Assignment Schedule

Day 1

1. Read New Structure—Summarizing Multiple References.
2. Your assignment is to prepare to write a paragraph about food the Roanoke people ate. That is why *Roanoke, people, food* are on the Roman numeral line (the topic line) of the source and fused outlines.
3. Read and discuss "The Roanoke People."
4. Reread the source text and put marks by three to five facts that are most interesting or important. These are facts that support the topic.
5. Write the facts on the first source outline.

Day 2

1. Read and discuss "Who Lived on Roanoke Island?"
2. Reread the source text and put marks by three to five facts that are most interesting or important. These are facts that support the topic. Do not mark facts that you already included from the first source.
3. Write the facts on the second source outline.

Day 3

1. Look at the vocabulary cards for Lesson 21. Complete Vocabulary Practice.
2. Review your source outlines. Choose five to six facts from the source outlines and write them on the fused outline.
3. Test your fused outline. If a note is unclear, check the source text and fix your fused outline.

Unit 6

In this new unit the KWO is formed by taking key words from interesting and important facts, similar to Unit 4. In this unit students receive multiple sources related to each topic. For each topic students take 3–5 notes from each source to form a source outline. Using the source outlines, students combine the notes to form a fused outline. Help students limit which facts they choose.

The paragraph is about a specific topic and should follow the topic-clincher rule.

Exemplar

The Exemplars file contains a student's completed assignment for Lessons 21 and 22. The Exemplar is for the teacher and not intended to be used by the student.

See the blue page for download instructions.

UNIT 6: SUMMARIZING MULTIPLE REFERENCES

Day 4

1. Review the vocabulary words and their meanings.

2. After practicing, use your fused outline to give an oral report to a friend or family member. Read. Think. Look up. Speak. If applicable, be prepared to give an oral report in class.

Read this page to introduce the new structural unit, Unit 6: Summarizing Multiple References. Like Unit 4, students take notes from the source text to write a report. Because there are two source texts, students will take notes from both texts and then fuse them into one KWO. Students will write from the fused outline.

Lesson 21: Roanoke, Part 1

New Structure

Summarizing Multiple References

In Unit 6 you will again write reports. Remember when you write a report your facts must be organized into paragraphs. Just like Unit 4 you will find the facts to support the topic in the source texts. This time you will use more than one source.

Each paragraph begins with a topic sentence, contain facts, and ends with a clincher sentence.

1 topic = 1 paragraph

Topic Sentence

> The topic sentence tells what the paragraph is about. When you write the KWO, ask yourself, "What will the paragraph be about?" The key words on the Roman numeral line of the source outlines and the fused outline state the topic.

Facts

> Gather facts by writing source outlines. Create one source outline for each source text. Once you have chosen your topic, read each of your sources and look for interesting or important facts that support the topic.

> Organize facts by writing a fused outline. Choose five to six facts from the source outlines and write them on the fused outline.

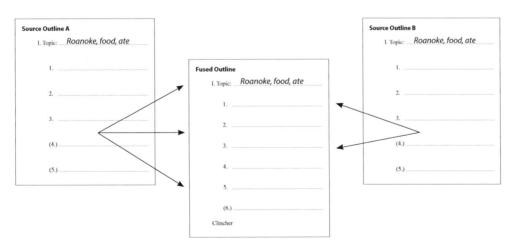

Clincher Sentence

> The clincher sentence reminds the reader what the paragraph was about. The fused outline ends with the word *clincher*.

Adventures in Writing: Student Book

Native Americans lived on Roanoke Island long before the English came to America in 1587. This small island, protected from the Atlantic Ocean by barrier islands, is located off the coast of North Carolina. Maize is another word for corn.

UNIT 6: SUMMARIZING MULTIPLE REFERENCES

Source Text A

The Roanoke People

The Roanoke people lived on a small island where they farmed and fished. They would carve huge canoes so that twenty men could fish together. They used nets and spears. At night they lit fires in their canoes. The fire attracted the fish so that the fishermen could then easily spear them. Sometimes they cooked their fish with vegetables in a clay pot and made stew. The Roanoke people grew vegetables in mounds, not rows. They planted corn, beans, and squash seeds together. They called these plants the three sisters because they helped each other as they grew together. The corn supported the beans and squash as they climbed the cornstalks. The beans put nitrogen in the dirt. The nitrogen from the beans helped the plants grow. The squash shaded the dirt and kept the bugs away.

The first English colonists learned how to fish and farm from the Roanoke people.

Source Text B

Who Lived on Roanoke Island?

The Native Americans who lived on Roanoke Island were peaceful people. They lived off the land. They made tea and medicines from sassafras and milkweed. They also grew pumpkins, beans, and gourds. Their most important crop was maize. These people were also fishermen. They hollowed out trees with shells and stone tools to make canoes. The fishermen built stone weirs to trap fish. Fish that swam into the weir could not find their way out. Using spears and nets, the fishermen scooped up fish. Sometimes these Native Americans ate inside their longhouses. Other times they ate outside. The women placed woven mats on the ground and served fish, vegetables, or other food on wooden platters. Men sat on one side, and women sat on the other. They did not use utensils. Instead, they ate with their hands.

UNIT 6: SUMMARIZING MULTIPLE REFERENCES

Students must limit which facts they choose to note. Help them look for the most interesting or most important facts that best explain the food the Roanoke people ate.

Next to the first Roman numeral, notice *Roanoke (subject), food (topic), ate* (one more word *about the topic*).

UNIT 6: SUMMARIZING MULTIPLE REFERENCES

Sample

Source Outlines

The assigned topic for this paragraph is food the Roanoke people ate. The titles of the source texts are on the Source line. The assigned topic is written in key words on the Roman numeral topic lines. Look at the source texts and note three to five interesting or important facts about the topic.

1 paragraph = 1 topic

Topic: *food*

Source A: "The Roanoke People"

I. Topic: _Roanoke, food, ate_

  1. _20 🧍, 🐟, together, canoe_

  2. _🌙, fires, canoes, attract, 🐟_

  3. _corn, beans, squash_

  (4.) _3 sisters, help, together_

  (5.) _____

Source B: "Who Lived on Roanoke Island?"

I. Topic: _Roanoke, food, ate_

  1. _🐚, stones, hollow, canoe_

  2. _stone weirs, trap, 🐟_

  3. _fish in, X out_

  (4.) _spears, nets_

  (5.) _____

Institute for Excellence in Writing

The topic on the source and fused outlines is identical. This is because students choose a topic to write about and then gather facts from both sources about the chosen topic. Only the fused outline has a clincher line because students write the paragraph using the fused outline.

Sample

Fused Outline

Lesson 21: Roanoke, Part 1

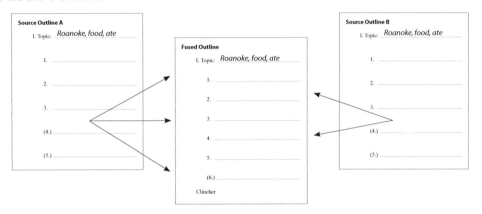

Select five to six facts from the source outlines to transfer to the fused outline.

I. Topic: _Roanoke, food, ate_

1. Source A → _corn, beans, squash_

2. Source A → _3 sisters, help, together_

3. _🐚, stones, hollow, canoe_ ← Source B

4. Source A → _20 🧍, 🐟, together, canoe_

5. Source A → _🌙, fires, canoes, attract, 🐟_

(6.) _stone weirs, trap, 🐟_ ← Source B

Clincher

Tell back the facts on the fused outline in complete sentences. Fix any notes you do not understand. For the clincher, repeat or reflect two or three key words from the topic line.

Fused Outline

Help students choose facts from both source outlines and place them in an order that makes sense.

Do not require students to indicate which source outline each note came from. This is just a visual for teachers.

UNIT 6: SUMMARIZING MULTIPLE REFERENCES

Vocabulary Practice

Listen   to someone read the vocabulary words for Lesson 21 aloud.

Speak   them aloud yourself.

Read   the definitions and sample sentences on the vocabulary cards.

Write   the part of speech and the definition beside the word.

skilled

adjective; trained or experienced to do something well

weir

noun; a small dam in a river or stream

Think   about the words. Can you use them in your report?

Lesson 22: Roanoke, Part 2

Structure: Unit 6: Summarizing Multiple References
Style: no new style
Subject: the Roanoke people

UNIT 6: SUMMARIZING MULTIPLE REFERENCES

Lesson 22: Roanoke, Part 2

Goals
- to write a 1-paragraph report
- to use new vocabulary words: *construct, nutritious*

Assignment Schedule

Day 1
1. Play Two Strikes and You're Out.
2. Review New Structure—Summarizing Multiple References from Lesson 21.
3. Review your fused outline from Lesson 21.
4. Say the topic-clincher rule.
5. Use the words on the topic line to write your topic sentence.
6. Complete Style Practice.

Day 2
1. Begin writing your rough draft. Use your KWO.
2. Look at the checklist. Check each box as you complete each requirement.

Day 3
1. Look at the vocabulary cards for Lesson 22. Complete Vocabulary Practice.
2. Practice saying the topic-clincher rule.
3. Finish writing your rough draft. Use your KWO and the checklist.
4. Turn in your rough draft to your editor with the completed checklist attached.

Day 4
1. Review the vocabulary words and their meanings.
2. Write or type a final draft.
3. Highlight or bold the key words *Roanoke, people, food* in the topic and clincher sentences.
4. Paperclip the checklist, final draft, rough draft, and KWO together.

Unit 6

In this lesson students use the fused outline created in Lesson 21 to write a paragraph.

The paragraph is about a specific topic, the food that Roanoke people ate, and should follow the topic-clincher rule.

Adventures in Writing: Student Book

UNIT 6: SUMMARIZING MULTIPLE REFERENCES

Style Practice

-ly Adverb Dress-Up

You must include an -ly adverb in the report you write.

What -ly adverbs could express how the fishermen built weirs?

usually, cleverly, carefully

Strong Verb Dress-Up

Do not use the exact words found in the text. On the line below each sentence, write strong verbs that are synonyms of the italicized words. Use a thesaurus.

1. The Roanoke people *cooked* fish and vegetables.

    strong verbs *grilled, simmered, prepared*

2. They *made* canoes.

    strong verbs *produced, constructed, formed*

Quality Adjective Dress-Up

Next to each noun, write ideas for adjectives that create a strong image and feeling. Avoid banned adjectives.

1. fishermen *clever, skilled, creative*

2. stew *delicious, nutritious, tasty*

Who/Which Clause Dress-Up

Add a *who/which* clause. Punctuate and mark correctly.

1. The farmers **, who lived on Roanoke Island,** planted seeds in mounds.

2. The fishermen built weirs **, which trapped fish.**

Because Clause Dress-Up

Add a *because* clause. Underline the word *because*.

1. The fishermen lit fires in their canoes because **fire attracted the fish.**

2. The women placed woven mats on the ground because **they served food on the ground.**

Look at your KWO and consider dress-ups to include in your report.

UNIT 6: SUMMARIZING MULTIPLE REFERENCES

Vocabulary Practice

Listen to someone read the vocabulary words for Lesson 22 aloud.

Speak them aloud yourself.

Read the definitions and sample sentences on the vocabulary cards.

Write two sentences using one of this lesson's vocabulary words in each sentence. You may use derivatives of the words.

construct _____

The fishermen constructed canoes.

_____

nutritious _____

The women cooked nutritious fish and

vegetable stew.

Think about the words. Can you use them in your report?

Lesson 22: Roanoke, Part 2

Unit 6 Composition Checklist
Lesson 22: Roanoke

Summarizing Multiple References

Name: _____

STRUCTURE
- ☐ name and date in upper left-hand corner _____ 2 pts
- ☐ composition double-spaced _____ 3 pts
- ☐ title centered and repeats 1–3 key words from final sentence _____ 10 pts
- ☐ topic-clincher sentences repeat or reflect 2–3 key words (highlight or bold) _____ 10 pts
- ☐ checklist on top, final draft, rough draft, key word outline _____ 10 pts

STYLE
¶1 ¶2 **Dress-Ups** (underline one of each)
- ☐ -ly adverb _____ 5 pts
- ☐ *who/which* clause _____ 5 pts
- ☐ strong verb _____ 5 pts
- ☐ *because* clause _____ 5 pts
- ☐ quality adjective _____ 5 pts

CHECK FOR BANNED WORDS (-1 pt for each use):
say/said, see/saw, go/went, good, bad _____ pts

MECHANICS
- ☐ capitalization _____ 10 pts
- ☐ end marks and punctuation _____ 10 pts
- ☐ complete sentences _____ 10 pts
- ☐ correct spelling _____ 10 pts

VOCABULARY
- ☐ vocabulary words - label *(voc)* in left margin or after sentence

Total: _____ 100 pts
Custom Total: _____ pts

Adventures in Writing: Student Book

Checklist

Teachers are free to adjust a checklist by requiring only the stylistic techniques that have become easy, plus one new one. EZ+1

Lesson 23: Mayflower, Part 1

Structure: Unit 6: Summarizing Multiple References
Style: no new style
Subject: the *Mayflower*

UNIT 6: SUMMARIZING MULTIPLE REFERENCES

Lesson 23: Mayflower, Part 1

Goals

- to practice the Unit 6 structural model
- to create source outlines from multiple references
- to create two fused outlines
- to use new vocabulary words: *cramped, shiver*

Assignment Schedule

Day 1

1. Play Vocabulary Find the Card.
2. Review New Structure—Identifying the Topic from Lesson 15.
3. Read and discuss "The Mayflower" and "Crossing the Atlantic."
4. Complete Structure Practice.

Day 2

1. Write the key words for *Mayflower's* description, the topic of your first paragraph, on the topic line of the source and fused outlines.
2. Write source outlines.
3. Choose facts from the source outlines and write the fused outline.

Day 3

1. Look at the vocabulary cards for Lesson 23. Complete Vocabulary Practice.
2. Write the key words for *Mayflower's* voyage, the topic of your second paragraph, on the topic line of the source and fused outlines.
3. Write source outlines.
4. Choose facts from the source outlines and write the fused outline.

Day 4

1. Review the vocabulary words and their meanings.
2. After practicing, use one of your fused outlines to give an oral report to a friend or family member. Read. Think. Look up. Speak.

Unit 6

In this lesson students will plan to write two paragraphs about two different topics. They again receive multiple sources related to each topic.

For each topic students take 3–5 notes from each source to form a source outline. Using the source outlines, students combine the notes to form a fused outline. Help students limit which facts they choose.

Each paragraph is about a specific topic and should follow the topic-clincher rule.

Adventures in Writing: Student Book

Read the first paragraph and ask students what the paragraph is about. It is a description of the small ship. The topic is *description*.

Source Text A

The Mayflower

The *Mayflower* was a small ship that carried 102 passengers and thirty sailors across the Atlantic in 1620. It was one hundred feet long and twenty-four feet wide. The ship had three masts. The lowest level of the ship was called the hold. Supplies were stored in the hold. The Pilgrims would need food, drink, tools, seeds, and animals in the New World. The next level of the ship was called the gun deck. This is where the passengers lived. The ceiling in that space was only five feet tall, so tall people could not stand up straight. There were no windows. The ship was designed to take cargo on short trips. It was not designed to take that many people on a three-thousand-mile journey across the Atlantic Ocean in the chilly fall weather.

Read the second paragraph and ask students what the paragraph is about. It is details about the voyage. The topic is *voyage*.

Lesson 23: Mayflower, Part 1

On September 6, 1620, the ship, its crew, and passengers left Plymouth, England. Their original plan was to leave for the New World in August, but they had to turn back twice. The weather was brutal. The passengers were cold and wet. They became seasick. Because the sailors did not want the passengers to fall into the ocean, they were rarely allowed on the upper deck. They had to stay in their tight, dark living quarters. One passenger who went to the upper deck was swept overboard by a huge wave. Thankfully, he grabbed a rope and was rescued. The only food they had was hard biscuits and salty meat. They did not have fresh water to drink. They only had beer. These difficulties caused many to become sick. The journey was slow. Sometimes strong winds pushed the ship backwards for days. After sixty-six days the Pilgrims finally arrived in America on November 11, 1620.

Mechanics

Italicize names of ships. If a report is handwritten, underline the ship name.

Read the first paragraph and ask students what the paragraph is about. It is a description of the small ship. The topic is *description*.

UNIT 6: SUMMARIZING MULTIPLE REFERENCES

Source Text B

Crossing the Atlantic

The *Mayflower* was a small ship that sailed across the Atlantic Ocean. It carried a group of Pilgrims, who were English men, women, and children, from England to America. The ship was not very long. It was about as long as a basketball court. The *Mayflower* had a lower deck called the hold, where the Pilgrims and the crew stored cargo. Farm tools, seeds, and animals such as chickens, sheep, and goats were kept there. The deck above the hold was called the gun deck. It usually stored cannons. This was where the Pilgrims slept and where they stored a thirty-foot boat, which they would use when they arrived in the New World. The crew worked on the upper deck. The crowded ship was not designed to carry so many people on a long journey.

The *Mayflower* had a long and dangerous voyage. The ocean was rough. The huge waves caused the ship to rock. Passengers became seasick. It smelled terrible. There was no fresh air on their small dark deck. During stormy weather

Read the second paragraph and ask students what the paragraph is about. It is details about the voyage. The topic is *voyage*.

Lesson 23: Mayflower, Part 1

lighting a fire on the wooden ship was dangerous. They could not have a hot meal, and they were hungry for something other than hardtack and salty fish. On their journey a large beam cracked. They wondered if they should go back to England. However, they were able to prop up the beam with an enormous iron screw. The Pilgrims' courage and dreams of a better life helped them survive their difficult passage.

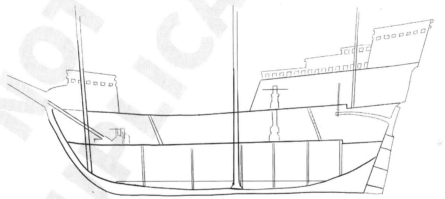

Structure Practice
Identifying the Topic
Now that you have read the source texts, fill in these blanks.

1. The subject for this lesson is _____Mayflower_____

2. Topics include _____description, voyage_____

3. On the source and fused outlines, write the topics on the topic lines following this pattern: *subject*, *topic*, one more word *about the topic*.

Subjects and Topics

The subject is *Mayflower*.

The topics are *description* and *voyage*, which are the divisions of the subject *Mayflower*. If necessary, tell students what to write in the blanks.

One more word *about the topic* is a descriptive word that narrows the topic. At this level, students can write any adjective that describes the topic.

Remind students of the pattern for the topic line: *subject*, *topic*, one more word *about the topic*. At this level, students can write any adjective that describes the topic. Instead of *crowded*, students might choose words like *cramped*, *small*, or *packed*.

Guide students to choose 3–5 facts from each source text related to the description of the ship.

UNIT 6: SUMMARIZING MULTIPLE REFERENCES

Sample

Source Outlines

Next to the first Roman numeral, write *Mayflower (subject)*, *description (topic)*. Think of one word to describe the description. Add this word to the topic line. Re-read the source text and write three to five facts to support the topic.

1 paragraph = 1 topic

Topic: description

Source A: "The Mayflower"

I. Topic: __Mayflower, description, crowded__

    1. __small, 100 ft X 24 ft, 102 passengers, 30 sailors__

    2. __↓ hold, tools, seeds__

    3. __gun deck, passengers, lived__

    (4.) __ceiling, 5 ft, X windows__

    (5.) __X designed, ++ people → Atlantic__

Source B: "Crossing the Atlantic"

I. Topic: __Mayflower, description, crowded__

    1. __Pilgrims, England → America__

    2. __X long, 🏀 court__

    3. __gun deck, cannons, P, slept__

    (4.) __30 ft ⛵, use, New World__

    (5.) _____

Make sure the words on the topic line of the source and fused outlines are identical.

Only the fused outline has a clincher line because students write the paragraph using the fused outline.

Sample

Lesson 23: Mayflower, Part 1

Fused Outline

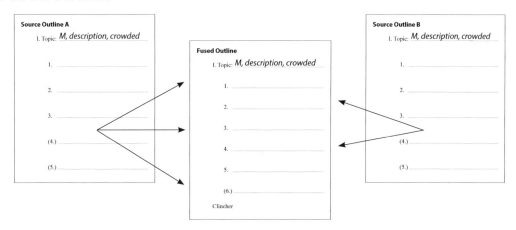

Select five to six facts from the source outlines to transfer to the fused outline.

I. Topic: _____Mayflower, description, crowded_____

1. _____100 ft X 24 ft, 🏀 court, 102 passengers, 30 sailors_____

2. _____↓ hold, tools, seeds_____

3. _____gun deck, cannons, P, slept_____

4. _____30 ft 🚢, use, New World_____

5. _____ceiling, 5 ft, X windows_____

(6.) _____X designed, ++ people → Atlantic_____

Clincher

Tell back the facts on the fused outline in complete sentences. Fix any notes you do not understand. For the clincher, repeat or reflect two or three key words from the topic line.

UNIT 6: SUMMARIZING MULTIPLE REFERENCES

> Remind students of the pattern for the topic line: *subject, topic,* one more word *about the topic.* Since the entire paper is about the *Mayflower,* the subject of this paragraph is the same as the subject of the first paragraph. The topic differs because each paragraph is about a specific topic. At this level, students can write any adjective that describes the topic. Instead of *difficult,* students might choose words like *hard, tough, painful,* or *unpleasant.*
>
> Guide students to choose 3–5 facts from each source text related to the voyage.

UNIT 6: SUMMARIZING MULTIPLE REFERENCES

Sample

Source Outlines

Next to the second Roman numeral, write *Mayflower (subject), voyage (topic).*
Think of one word to describe the voyage. Add this word to the topic line.
Re-read the source text and write three to five facts to support the topic.

1 paragraph = 1 topic

Topic: voyage

Source A: "The Mayflower"

II. Topic: _Mayflower, voyage, difficult_

   1. _9/6/1620, Plymouth, England → America_

   2. _back, 2X, weather, brutal_

   3. _cold, wet, sick_

  (4.) _X fresh, H_2O_

  (5.) _66 d, P, arrived, America, 11/11/1620_

Source B: "Crossing the Atlantic"

II. Topic: _Mayflower, voyage, difficult_

   1. _〰️ rough, rock, seasick_

   2. _X fresh air, X hot 🍲_

   3. _hungry, hardtack, salty ∝_

  (4.) _courage, dream, survived_

  (5.) _____

Make sure the words on the topic line of the source and fused outlines are identical.

Only the fused outline has a clincher line because students write the paragraph using the fused outline.

Sample

Lesson 23: Mayflower, Part 1

Fused Outline

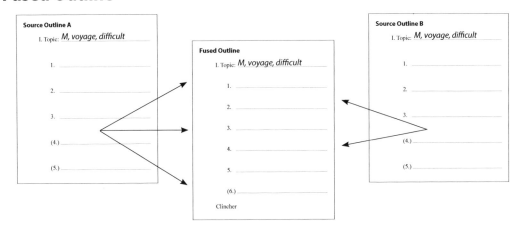

Select five to six facts from the source outlines to transfer to the fused outline.

II. Topic: _Mayflower, voyage, difficult_

1. _9/6/1620, Plymouth, England → America_

2. _back, 2X, weather, brutal_

3. _cold, wet, sick_

4. _X fresh H_2O, air_

5. _hungry, hardtack, salty ∝_

(6.) _66 d, P, arrived, America, 11/11/1620_

Clincher

Tell back the facts on the fused outline in complete sentences. Fix any notes you do not understand. For the clincher, repeat or reflect two or three key words from the topic line.

UNIT 6: SUMMARIZING MULTIPLE REFERENCES

Vocabulary Practice

Listen   to someone read the vocabulary words for Lesson 23 aloud.

Speak   them aloud yourself.

Read   the definitions and sample sentences on the vocabulary cards.

Write   the correct words in the blanks. You may use derivatives of the words.

Passengers lived in the _____*cramped*_____ gun deck.

The Pilgrims _____*shivered*_____ in their chilly living quarters.

Think   about the words. Can you use them in your report?

Lesson 24: Mayflower, Part 2

Structure: Unit 6: Summarizing Multiple References
Style: *www.asia* clause
Subject: the *Mayflower*

UNIT 6: SUMMARIZING MULTIPLE REFERENCES

Lesson 24: Mayflower, Part 2

Goals

- to write a 2-paragraph report
- to add a new dress-up: *www.asia* clause
- to review vocabulary words

Assignment Schedule

Day 1

1. Play the Question Game.
2. Review your fused outlines from Lesson 23.
3. Read New Style and complete Style Practice.

Day 2

1. Say the topic-clincher rule.
2. Write a rough draft for your first paragraph.
3. Highlight or bold the key words *Mayflower, description, + word* in the topic and clincher sentences.

Day 3

1. Complete Vocabulary Review.
2. Write a rough draft for your second paragraph.
3. Highlight or bold the key words *Mayflower, voyage, + word* in the topic and clincher sentences.
4. Look at the checklist. Check each box as you complete each requirement.
5. Turn in your rough draft to your editor with the completed checklist attached.

Day 4

1. Study for Vocabulary Quiz 5. It will cover words from Lessons 20–23.
2. Write or type a final draft.
3. Paperclip the checklist, final draft, rough draft, and KWO together.

Unit 6

In this lesson students use the fused outlines created in Lesson 23 to write two paragraphs.

Each paragraph is about a specific topic and should follow the topic-clincher rule.

Question Game

See Appendix IV for game directions. For this lesson use questions 1–28 and vocabulary words.

UNIT 6: SUMMARIZING MULTIPLE REFERENCES

A *www.asia* clause contains both a subject and a verb.

As a Pilgrim is not a clause because *As a Pilgrim* does not contain a subject and a verb.

As a Pilgrim is a prepositional phrase.

As Pilgrims journeyed across the water is a clause because *As Pilgrims journeyed across the water* contains a subject (*Pilgrims*) and a verb (*journeyed*).

Recite the seven www words and the pattern (www word + subject + verb) over and over with students.

www.asia Clause

At this level, teach students to place the *www.asia* clause after a sentence that is already complete.

As students become more sophisticated in their writing, they will learn that the *because* clause and the *www.asia* clause are both adverb clauses and have two comma rules.

Use a comma after an adverb clause that comes before a main clause.

AC, MC

Do not use a comma before an adverb clause.

MC AC

At this level, require students to place the *www.asia* clause after a main clause. No comma is needed.

UNIT 6: SUMMARIZING MULTIPLE REFERENCES

New Style

www.asia Clause Dress-Up

In this lesson you will learn the final dress-up: *www.asia* clause.

A *www.asia* clause is a group of words that begins with a www word and contains a subject and a verb. Use the acronym *www.asia* to learn the seven most common www words: *when, while, where, as, since, if, although*.

www word + subject + verb

The ship left <u>when</u> the weather was chilly.

The Pilgrims became sick <u>since</u> they had no fresh air.

Notice:

1. A *www.asia* clause begins with a www word.

    To indicate a *www.asia* clause, underline the www word.

2. A *www.asia* clause contains a subject and a verb.

    The ship left <u>when</u> the *weather was* chilly.

    The Pilgrims became sick <u>since</u> *they had* no fresh air.

3. A *www.asia* clause is added to a sentence that is already complete.

    The ship left <u>when</u> the weather was chilly.

    The Pilgrims became sick <u>since</u> they had no fresh air.

 Do not use a comma before a *www.asia* clause.

The ship left <u>when</u> the weather was chilly.

From now on, include a *www.asia* clause in each paragraph you write.
Mark the *www.asia* clause by underlining the www word.

Style Practice

www.asia Clause Dress-Up

Add a *www.asia* clause. Underline the www word.

The Pilgrims did not give up <u>although</u> they became sick.

Because Clause Dress-Up

Write two sentences with a *because* clause that you could use in your report.
Add the clause to a sentence that is already complete. Punctuate and mark correctly.

Tall passengers could not stand up <u>because</u> the ceiling was too short.

The Pilgrims became seasick <u>because</u> the ship rocked.

Who/Which Clause Dress-Up

Write two sentences with a *who/which* clause that you could use in your report.
Punctuate and mark correctly.

The Mayflower, <u>which</u> had three masts, carried too many passengers.

The Pilgrims, <u>who</u> lived in the crowded ship, finally reached America.

---

www.asia Clause

- Read the main clause. Point out that it is a complete sentence.
- Read the main clause again and ask, "Why?"
- Orally fill in the blank several times with various answers.
- When students understand the pattern of the *www.asia* clause, direct them to write.

UNIT 6: SUMMARIZING MULTIPLE REFERENCES

Quality Adjective Dress-Up

Next to each noun, write ideas for adjectives that create a strong image and feeling. Avoid banned adjectives.

1. ship *tiny, cramped, tight, smelly*

2. Pilgrims *scared, hungry, hopeful, discouraged*

Look at your KWO and consider dress-ups to include in your report.

Vocabulary Review

Listen to someone read the vocabulary words for Lessons 20–23 aloud.

Speak them aloud yourself.

Read the definitions and sample sentences on the vocabulary cards.

Write the words that match the definitions.

cramped — too small and crowded

discover — to find

weir — a small dam in a river or stream

nutritious — promoting good health and growth

skilled — trained or experienced to do something well

shiver — to shake or tremble with cold, fear, or excitement

delicate — easily damaged

construct — to build or make something

Lesson 24: Mayflower, Part 2

Unit 6 Composition Checklist
Lesson 24: Mayflower

Summarizing Multiple References

Name: _____

STRUCTURE
- ☐ name and date in upper left-hand corner _____ 2 pts
- ☐ composition double-spaced _____ 3 pts
- ☐ title centered and repeats 1–3 key words from final sentence _____ 5 pts
- ☐ topic-clincher sentences repeat or reflect 2–3 key words (highlight or bold) _____ 10 pts
- ☐ checklist on top, final draft, rough draft, key word outline _____ 4 pts

STYLE
¶1 ¶2 **Dress-Ups** (underline one of each) (3 pts each)
- ☐ ☐ *-ly* adverb _____ 6 pts
- ☐ ☐ *who/which* clause _____ 6 pts
- ☐ ☐ strong verb _____ 6 pts
- ☐ ☐ *because* clause _____ 6 pts
- ☐ ☐ quality adjective _____ 6 pts
- ☐ ☐ *www.asia* clause _____ 6 pts

CHECK FOR BANNED WORDS (-1 pt for each use):
say/said, see/saw, go/went, good, bad _____ pts

MECHANICS
- ☐ capitalization _____ 10 pts
- ☐ end marks and punctuation _____ 10 pts
- ☐ complete sentences _____ 10 pts
- ☐ correct spelling _____ 10 pts

VOCABULARY
- ☐ vocabulary words - label *(voc)* in left margin or after sentence

Total: _____ 100 pts
Custom Total: _____ pts

Checklist

Teachers are free to adjust a checklist by requiring only the stylistic techniques that have become easy, plus one new one. EZ+1

Lesson 25: William Penn, Part 1

Structure: Unit 6: Summarizing Multiple References
Style: no new style
Subject: William Penn

UNIT 6: SUMMARIZING MULTIPLE REFERENCES

Lesson 25: William Penn, Part 1

Goals

- to practice the Unit 6 structural model
- to create source outlines from multiple references
- to create two fused outlines
- to take Vocabulary Quiz 5
- to use new vocabulary words: *expel, illegal*

Assignment Schedule

Day 1

1. Play Find the *www.asia* Clause Starters.
2. Take Vocabulary Quiz 5.
3. Read and discuss "William Penn" and "The Founding of Pennsylvania."
4. Complete Structure Practice.

Day 2

1. Write source outlines for William Penn's early life.
2. Choose facts from the source outlines and write the fused outline.

Day 3

1. Look at the vocabulary cards for Lesson 25. Complete Vocabulary Practice.
2. Write source outlines for William Penn's planning of Philadelphia.
3. Choose facts from the source outlines and write the fused outline.

Day 4

1. Review the vocabulary words and their meanings.
2. After practicing, use one of your fused outlines to give an oral report to a friend or family member. Read. Think. Look up. Speak.

Adventures in Writing: Student Book

Read the first paragraph and ask students what the paragraph is about. It is about William Penn's early life. The topic is *early life*.

Source Text A

William Penn

William Penn spent his early life in England. He was born on October 13, 1644, in a neighborhood near the Tower of London. When William Penn was three years old, he had smallpox. The disease caused him to lose all his hair, so he wore a wig until he went to college. Penn and his family moved from London to Essex, a town in the country. This is where he learned to love nature. When he was twelve, his family moved to Ireland, where he learned about the Quakers. Quakers were not respected by the Church of England, and there were laws against their religion. William Penn attended Oxford College and thought he might want to be a doctor or a politician. However, after two years he was asked to leave because he was a Quaker. He was arrested many times and was sent to jail. He did not stay in jail because his father, Sir William Penn, was a wealthy and important man. After his father died, he received the land of Pennsylvania, where he had freedom to be a Quaker.

> Read the second paragraph and ask students what the paragraph is about. It is about Philadelphia. The topic is *Philadelphia*.

The town of Philadelphia was a part of William Penn's plan for Pennsylvania. The name came from two Greek words, *philos*, meaning love, and *adelphos*, meaning brotherhood. Penn wanted the city of brotherly love to have straight and wide streets. He named the streets with numbers and names of trees. The streets ran north and south or east and west, creating a grid pattern. Many lots became parks and public places. Trees and gardens surrounded every house. After he planned the town, he wrote to his Quaker friends and invited them to buy land. By 1684 four thousand people lived in Philadelphia. Pennsylvania became a successful American colony, and the city of Philadelphia became the pattern for many cities across America.

Mechanics

Capitalize titles that come directly before a name or a country.

Capitalize *north*, *south*, *east*, and *west* when they refer to a region or proper name. Do not capitalize these words when they indicate direction.

Read the first paragraph and ask students what the paragraph is about. It is about William Penn's early life. The topic is *early life*.

UNIT 6: SUMMARIZING MULTIPLE REFERENCES

Source Text B

The Founding of Pennsylvania

William Penn was born to a wealthy family in 1644 in London, England. His father, Sir William Penn, was a respected admiral in the English navy. His mother was the daughter of a rich Dutch merchant. When William Penn was a young boy, his family moved to the countryside in Essex. Penn loved the outdoors and often ran more than three miles from his home to school. As part of a wealthy family, he received an excellent education. When he attended university, he became a Quaker. This upset his father. After his father died, William Penn asked the King of England to give him land in America in exchange for the debt the king owed his family. Penn wanted the land so that he and other Quakers could be free to worship as they wanted. The king gave him the land in 1681 and named it Pennsylvania, which means "Penn's woods."

Read the second paragraph and ask students what the paragraph is about. It is about Philadelphia. The topic is *Philadelphia*.

Lesson 25: William Penn, Part 1

William Penn had a plan for Philadelphia, the capital of Pennsylvania. Penn chose the name Philadelphia because it means the city of brotherly love. He thought about the crooked and crowded streets of London and wanted something more open for Philadelphia. He wanted straight and wide streets. He wanted the homes to have lawns and gardens. He wanted large plots of land to be used for parks and city buildings. In this town people could worship God freely. William Penn was very pleased with the new town of Philadelphia. He called it the green country town.

Structure Practice
Identifying the Topic
Now that you have read the source texts, fill in these blanks.

1. The subject for this lesson is _William Penn_

2. Topics include _early life, Philadelphia_

3. On the source and fused outlines, write the topics on the topic lines following this pattern: *subject*, *topic*, one more word *about the topic*.

Adventures in Writing: Student Book

Subjects and Topics

The subject is *William Penn*.

The topics are *early life* and *Philadelphia*, which are the divisions of the subject *Penn*. If necessary, tell students what to write in the blanks.

One more word *about the topic* is a descriptive word that narrows the topic. At this level, students can write any adjective that describes the topic.

UNIT 6: SUMMARIZING MULTIPLE REFERENCES

A report is about one subject. Each paragraph is about a topic related to that subject. Both paragraphs will be about the subject *William Penn*. The topic of the first paragraph is early life. Help students add an adjective to the topic line that describes his *early life*. At this level, students can write any adjective that describes the topic. Instead of *eventful*, students might choose words like *interesting*, *fascinating*, or *memorable*.

Guide students to choose 3–5 facts from each source text related to Penn's early life.

Key Words

The term *early life* is a compound word and counts as one word on the KWO.

UNIT 6: SUMMARIZING MULTIPLE REFERENCES

Sample

Source Outlines

Next to the first Roman numeral, write *Penn (subject), early life (topic)*.
Think of one word to describe his early life. Add this word to the topic line.
Re-read the source text and write three to five facts to support the topic.

1 paragraph = 1 topic

Topic: early life

Source A: "William Penn"

I. Topic: _Penn, early life, eventful_

1. _3 yo, smallpox, X hair, wig_
2. _moved, Essex, ♡ nature_
3. _12 yo, Ireland, Quakers, illegal_
(4.) _leave, university, ++ arrests_
(5.) _received, PA, freedom, Quaker_

Source B: "The Founding of Pennsylvania"

I. Topic: _Penn, early life, eventful_

1. _b, 1644, London, England, wealthy_
2. _father, Sir William Penn, navy_
3. _♡, outdoors, ran > 3 mi, 🏠 → school_
(4.) _father, died, 👑 → PA, debt_
(5.) _WP + Quakers, free, worship_

Make sure the words on the topic line of the source and fused outlines are identical.

Only the fused outline has a clincher line because students write the paragraph using the fused outline.

Sample

Fused Outline

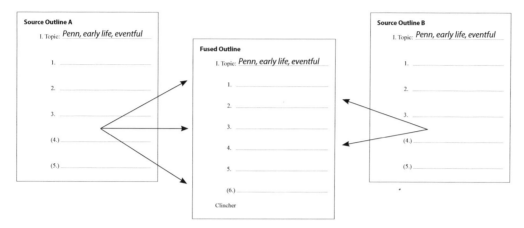

Select five to six facts from the source outlines to transfer to the fused outline.

I. Topic: _____ *Penn, early life, eventful* _____

1. _____ *b, 1644, London, wealthy, F, navy* _____

2. _____ *3 yo, smallpox, X hair, wig* _____

3. _____ *12 yo, Ireland, Quakers, illegal* _____

4. _____ *leave, university, ++ arrests* _____

5. _____ *father, died, ♛ → PA, debt* _____

(6.) _____ *WP + Quakers, free, worship* _____

Clincher

Tell back the facts on the fused outline in complete sentences. Fix any notes you do not understand. For the clincher, repeat or reflect two or three key words from the topic line.

186 UNIT 6: SUMMARIZING MULTIPLE REFERENCES

Remind students of the pattern for the topic line: *subject*, *topic*, one more word *about the topic*. Since the entire paper is about *William Penn*, the subject of this paragraph is the same as the subject of the first paragraph. The topic differs because each paragraph is about a specific topic. At this level, students can write any adjective that describes the topic. Instead of *planned* (a planned city), students might choose words like *arranged*, or *designed*.

Guide students to choose 3–5 facts from each source text related to Philadelphia.

UNIT 6: SUMMARIZING MULTIPLE REFERENCES

Sample

Source Outlines

Next to the second Roman numeral, write *Penn (subject)*, *Philadelphia (topic)*. Think of one word to describe Philadelphia. Add this word to the topic line. Re-read the source text and write three to five facts to support the topic.

1 paragraph = 1 topic

Topic: *Philadelphia*

Source A: "William Penn"

II. Topic: *Penn, Philadelphia, planned*

  1. *philos = ♡, adelphos = brotherhood*

  2. *N + S, E + W, grid, named, #s + trees*

  3. *++ trees, ++ parks*

  (4.) *invited, Quakers, 1684, 4,000 people*

  (5.) *successful, Am, colony, pattern*

Source B: "The Founding of Pennsylvania"

II. Topic: *Penn, Philadelphia, planned*

  1. *named, city, brotherly ♡*

  2. *straight, wide, streets*

  3. *++ gardens, parks, buildings*

  (4.) *free, worship, God*

  (5.) *WP, ☺, green country town*

Institute for Excellence in Writing

Make sure the words on the topic line of the source and fused outlines are identical.
Only the fused outline has a clincher line because students write the paragraph using the fused outline.

Sample

Lesson 25: William Penn, Part 1

Fused Outline

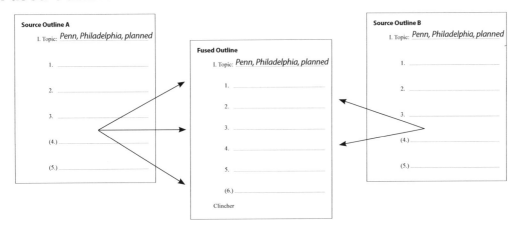

Select five to six facts from the source outlines to transfer to the fused outline.

II. Topic: _WP, Philadelphia, planned_

1. _philos = ♡, adelphos = brotherhood_

2. _straight, wide, streets_

3. _++ gardens, parks, buildings_

4. _free, worship, God_

5. _invited, Quakers, 1684, 4,000 people_

(6.) _successful, Am, colony, pattern_

Clincher

Tell back the facts on the fused outline in complete sentences. Fix any notes you do not understand. For the clincher, repeat or reflect two or three key words from the topic line.

UNIT 6: SUMMARIZING MULTIPLE REFERENCES

Vocabulary Practice

Listen   to someone read the vocabulary words for Lesson 25 aloud.

Speak   them aloud yourself.

Read   the definitions and sample sentences on the vocabulary cards.

Write   the part of speech and the definition beside the word.

expel

verb; to force someone to leave a place

illegal

adjective; not allowed by law

Think   about the words. Can you use them in your report?

Lesson 26: William Penn, Part 2

Structure: Unit 6: Summarizing Multiple References
Style: no new style
Subject: William Penn

UNIT 6: SUMMARIZING MULTIPLE REFERENCES

Lesson 26: William Penn, Part 2

Goals

- to write a 2-paragraph report
- to use new vocabulary words: *design, desire*

Assignment Schedule

Day 1

1. Play Two Strikes and You're Out.
2. Review your fused outlines from Lesson 25.
3. Complete Style Practice.

Day 2

1. Say the topic-clincher rule.
2. Write a rough draft for your first paragraph.
3. Highlight or bold the key words *Penn, early life, + word* in the topic and clincher sentences.

Day 3

1. Look at the vocabulary cards for Lesson 26. Complete Vocabulary Practice.
2. Write a rough draft for your second paragraph.
3. Highlight or bold the key words *Penn, Philadelphia, + word* in the topic and clincher sentences.
4. Look at the checklist. Check each box as you complete each requirement.
5. Turn in your rough draft to your editor with the completed checklist attached.

Day 4

1. Review the vocabulary words and their meanings.
2. Write or type a final draft.
3. Paperclip the checklist, final draft, rough draft, and KWO together.

UNIT 6: SUMMARIZING MULTIPLE REFERENCES

Style Practice

Strong Verb Dress-Up and -ly Adverb Dress-Up

On the first line below the sentence, write strong verbs that could replace the italicized banned verb. On the second line write ideas for -ly adverbs that you could use with the strong verbs.

The Quakers *went* to Pennsylvania.

strong verbs _____ moved, traveled, journeyed _____

-ly adverbs _____ thankfully, joyfully, expectantly _____

Quality Adjective Dress-Up

Look at your KWO and list four different nouns that you could use in your report. Next to each noun, write ideas for adjectives that create a strong image and feeling. Avoid banned adjectives.

1. William Penn — bald, fast, intelligent

2. Philadelphia — peaceful, free, organized

3. Sir William Penn — prosperous, furious, generous

4. gardens — vast, beautiful, lush

Who/Which Clause Dress-Up

Combine the statements using the word *who* or *which*. Punctuate and mark correctly.

William Penn had smallpox. He lost all his hair.

William Penn, <u>who</u> had smallpox, lost all his hair.

William Penn had smallpox, <u>which</u> caused him to lose all his hair.

Because Clause Dress-Up

Add a *because* clause. Underline the word *because*.

William Penn was sent to jail *<u>because</u> he was a Quaker.*

www.asia Clause Dress-Up

Write the seven www words that can begin a *www.asia* clause.

when, while, where, as, since, if, although

www.asia Clause Dress-Up

Add a *www.asia* clause. Underline the www word.

The Quakers moved to Pennsylvania *<u>when</u> William Penn invited them.*

Look at your KWO and consider dress-ups to include in your report.

UNIT 6: SUMMARIZING MULTIPLE REFERENCES

Vocabulary Practice

Listen to someone read the vocabulary words for Lesson 26 aloud.

Speak them aloud yourself.

Read the definitions and sample sentences on the vocabulary cards.

Write two sentences using one of this lesson's vocabulary words in each sentence. You may use derivatives of the words.

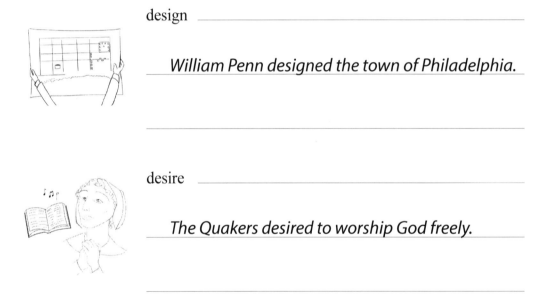

design _____

William Penn designed the town of Philadelphia.

_____

desire _____

The Quakers desired to worship God freely.

_____

Think about the words. Can you use them in your report?

Lesson 26: William Penn, Part 2

Unit 6 Composition Checklist
Lesson 26: William Penn

Summarizing Multiple References

Name: _____

STRUCTURE
- ☐ name and date in upper left-hand corner _____ 2 pts
- ☐ composition double-spaced _____ 3 pts
- ☐ title centered and repeats 1–3 key words from final sentence _____ 5 pts
- ☐ topic-clincher sentences repeat or reflect 2–3 key words (highlight or bold) _____ 10 pts
- ☐ checklist on top, final draft, rough draft, key word outline _____ 4 pts

STYLE
¶1 ¶2 **Dress-Ups** (underline one of each) (3 pts each)
- ☐ ☐ -ly adverb _____ 6 pts
- ☐ ☐ *who/which* clause _____ 6 pts
- ☐ ☐ strong verb _____ 6 pts
- ☐ ☐ *because* clause _____ 6 pts
- ☐ ☐ quality adjective _____ 6 pts
- ☐ ☐ *www.asia* clause _____ 6 pts

CHECK FOR BANNED WORDS (-1 pt for each use):
say/said, see/saw, go/went, good, bad _____ pts

MECHANICS
- ☐ capitalization _____ 10 pts
- ☐ end marks and punctuation _____ 10 pts
- ☐ complete sentences _____ 10 pts
- ☐ correct spelling _____ 10 pts

VOCABULARY
- ☐ vocabulary words - label *(voc)* in left margin or after sentence

Total: _____ 100 pts
Custom Total: _____ pts

Adventures in Writing: Student Book

Checklist

Teachers are free to adjust a checklist by requiring only the stylistic techniques that have become easy, plus one new one. EZ+1

Intentionally blank so the checklist can be removed.

Lesson 27: My House, Part 1

Preparation: *Teaching Writing: Structure and Style*
Watch the sections for Unit 7: Inventive Writing.
At IEW.com/twss-help reference the TWSS Viewing Guides.

Structure: Unit 7: Inventive Writing
Style: no new style
Subject: my house

UNIT 7: INVENTIVE WRITING

Lesson 27: My House, Part 1

Goals

- to learn the Unit 7 Inventive Writing structural model
- to create a KWO from a writing prompt
- to use new vocabulary words: *bond, store*

Assignment Schedule

Day 1

1. Play a game from the Teacher's Manual.
2. Read New Structure—Inventive Writing.
3. Read the prompt and complete the practice.
4. Read Notes from the Brain.

Day 2

1. Write a KWO about topic A, a room in your house.
2. Test your KWO and write a topic sentence.

Day 3

1. Look at the vocabulary cards for Lesson 27. Complete Vocabulary Practice.
2. Write a KWO about topic B, a different room in your house.
3. Test your KWO and write a topic sentence.

Day 4

1. Review the vocabulary words and their meanings.
2. After practicing, use your KWO to give an oral report to a friend or family member. Read. Think. Look up. Speak.

Unit 7

In this new unit students do not have a source text or even pictures to look at. The KWO is formed by asking good questions. Key words for the outline are found in the answers to the questions. Be patient with yourself and your students. This is a practicable skill that will take time to perfect.

Exemplar

The Exemplars file contains a student's completed assignment for Lessons 27 and 28. The Exemplar is for the teacher and not intended to be used by the student.

See the blue page for download instructions.

Remind students that the subject is the thing the entire paper is about. The topic is the division of or thing within the subject. In this assignment the subject *house* is assigned. Students must choose the topics.

UNIT 7: INVENTIVE WRITING

New Structure
Inventive Writing

In Unit 7 your entire composition should be about one subject. Once you know what the subject of the composition is, you determine how many paragraphs to write. Once you know the number of paragraphs, you determine the topics. Each paragraph equals one topic.

2 topics = 2 paragraphs

Subject

I. Topic A   *topic, 5–6 details, clincher*

II. Topic B   *topic, 5–6 details, clincher*

Prompt

Write two paragraphs about your house.

Practice

Because you must write two paragraphs about your house, you will choose two topics. List four different rooms in your house. Choose two.

The topic sentence will tell the topic of the paragraph. On the KWO write the subject and topic next to the Roman numeral. Follow this pattern.

I. *house, topic* A   II. *house, topic* B

Subjects and Topics

The topic line follows the pattern *subject, topic*, one more word *about the topic*.

For this assignment, the subject is *house*, and the topics are rooms in the house.

In the sample *topic A* is kitchen, and *topic B* is garage.

Each topic becomes one paragraph.

Notes from the Brain

You will write this paper without the help of source texts. Just like the other assignments, you must begin by writing a KWO.

To write the KWO, take notes from your brain. To do this, ask yourself questions. Use your answers to create the KWO.

Begin by memorizing these questions.

**who?   what?   when?
where?   why?   how?**

Describe the topic by asking yourself questions.

Who is with me in this room?

What do we do in this room?

When am I in this room?

Where is this room in my house?

Why do I like this room?

How do I feel about this room?

Draw a picture of your house.

The answers to your questions become the details for the outline. As you answer a question, write two or three key words on the KWO. Use symbols, numbers, and abbreviations when possible.

You do not have to answer every question. You do not need to ask the questions in the order they are written. Keep your answers short. You can add more details when you write your composition.

Repeat this process for the second topic.

2 topics = 2 paragraphs

198   UNIT 7: INVENTIVE WRITING

The topic line follows the pattern *subject, topic,* one more word *about the topic*. The one more word *about the topic* must be related to the topic. An adjective often works best. However, it does not have to be an adjective. In the sample, *meals* is the one more word. The facts are all about meals in the kitchen.

The key to the inventive writing process is asking questions. Here are the questions asked that resulted in the sample KWO.

UNIT 7: INVENTIVE WRITING

Sample

Key Word Outline

Next to the Roman numeral (the topic line), write the subject and topic. Follow this pattern: *house, topic A*. Think of one word to describe this room. Add this + *word* to the topic line.

Write five or six details about the topic.

Topic

What is the subject? *(house)*

What room in your house is this paragraph about? *(kitchen)*

What about the kitchen? *(meals)*

I.   Topic: _____ house, kitchen, meals _____   ?

1. _____ 1st level → living room _____   who?

Details

1. Where is this room?
2. What do you do in this room?
3–4. What do you prepare?
5. What else do you do in this room?
6. Who are you in this room with?

2. _____ help, mom, prepare _____   what?

3. _____ chop, veggies, salad _____   when?

4. _____ bake, muffins, cookies _____   where?

5. _____ set, table, pretty 🌷 _____   why?

(6.) _____ family, bond, stories ☺ _____   how?

Clincher

Clincher

Discuss ideas for a clincher sentence using two or three key words that repeat or reflect words written on the topic sentence line.

Here is a sample clincher sentence:

I love preparing **meals** *in the* **kitchen**, *which is my favorite room in my* **house**.

Test your KWO. For the clincher, repeat or reflect the words on the topic line.

Topic Sentence

The topic sentence tells what the paragraph is about. Use the key words on the topic line (or synonyms of those words) to write a topic sentence.

In my **house** *we eat* **meals** *in the* **kitchen**.

Institute for Excellence in Writing

Sample

Key Word Outline

Lesson 27: My House, Part 1

Next to the Roman numeral (the topic line), write the subject and topic. Follow this pattern: *house, topic B*. Think of one word to describe this room. Add this + *word* to the topic line.

Write five or six details about the topic.

II. Topic: _house, garage, useful_ ?

1. _attached, left, house_ — who?
2. _bike, skates, balls_ — what?
3. _chalk, bubbles_ — when?
4. _play, siblings, friends_ — where?
5. ☁ _mom, car, out_ — why?
(6.) _rollerblade, soccer_ — how?

Clincher

Test your KWO. For the clincher, repeat or reflect the words on the topic line.

Topic Sentence

The topic sentence tells what the paragraph is about. Use the key words on the topic line (or synonyms of those words) to write a topic sentence.

> The **garage** is a **useful** room in my **house**.

Topic

What is the subject? *(house)*

What room in your house is this paragraph about? *(garage)*

The garage is _____. What word describes the garage? *(useful)*

Details

1. Where is this room?
2–3. What is in this room?
4. Who are you in this room with?
5–6. What else do you do in this room?

Clincher

Discuss ideas for a clincher sentence using two or three key words that repeat or reflect words written on the topic sentence line.

Here is a sample clincher sentence:

*The **garage** attached to our **house** is **useful**.*

UNIT 7: INVENTIVE WRITING

Vocabulary Practice

Listen   to someone read the vocabulary words for Lesson 27 aloud.

Speak   them aloud yourself.

Read   the definitions and sample sentences on the vocabulary cards.

Write   the correct words in the blanks. You may use derivatives of the words.

I _____*bond*_____ with my family in my house.

We _____*store*_____ toys in this room.

Think   about the words. Can you use them in your composition?

Lesson 28: My House, Part 2

Structure: Unit 7: Inventive Writing
Style: no new style
Subject: my house

UNIT 7: INVENTIVE WRITING

Lesson 28: My House, Part 2

Goals

- to write a 2-paragraph composition
- to use new vocabulary words: *comfortable, spacious*

Assignment Schedule

Day 1

1. Play Find the *www.asia* Clause Starters.
2. Review your KWO from Lesson 27.
3. Complete Style Practice.

Day 2

1. Say the topic-clincher rule.
2. Write a rough draft for your first paragraph.
3. Highlight or bold the key words *house, topic A, + word* in the topic and clincher sentences.

Day 3

1. Look at the vocabulary cards for Lesson 28. Complete Vocabulary Practice.
2. Write a rough draft for your second paragraph.
3. Highlight or bold the key words *house, topic B, + word* in the topic and clincher sentences.
4. Look at the checklist. Check each box as you complete each requirement.
5. Turn in your rough draft to your editor with the completed checklist attached.

Day 4

1. Review the vocabulary words and their meanings.
2. Draw a picture to put with your composition.
3. Write or type a final draft.
4. Paperclip the checklist, picture, final draft, rough draft, and KWO together.

Unit 7

In this lesson students use the KWO created in Lesson 27 to write two paragraphs about their house.

Topic A is the first room written about and *topic B* is the second room written about. The *+ words* are about the specific rooms.

Students should follow the topic-clincher rule as practiced and modeled on pages 198–199.

UNIT 7: INVENTIVE WRITING

Style Practice
Strong Verb Dress-Up and -ly Adverb Dress-Up

Look at your KWO and write ideas for each.

Suggested Answers

The suggested answers work with the sample KWO.

Students' answers will depend upon chosen topics.

1. List strong verbs and -ly adverbs to include in your first paragraph.

   strong verbs — *bond, consume, prepare*

   -ly adverbs — *joyfully, hungrily, carefully*

2. List strong verbs and -ly adverbs to include in your second paragraph.

   strong verbs — *find, store, dash*

   -ly adverbs — *conveniently, easily, constantly*

Quality Adjective Dress-Up

Look at your KWO and list two different nouns that you could use in your composition. Next to each noun, write ideas for adjectives that create a strong image and feeling. Avoid banned adjectives.

1. *meals* — *delicious, nutritious, healthy*

2. *toys* — *messy, outdoor, favorite*

Who/Which Clause Dress-Up

Write two sentences with a *who/which* clause that you could use in your composition.

In the kitchen we enjoy meals, <u>which</u> I help my mom cook.

The garage is attached to the left of my home, <u>which</u> sits on a quiet street.

Because Clause Dress-Up

Write two sentences with a *because* clause that you could use in your composition.

I help my mom prepare nutritious meals <u>because</u> I love to cook and bake.

We store balls in the garage <u>because</u> we can easily find them to play outside.

www.asia Clause Dress-Up

Write two sentences with a *www.asia* clause that you could use in your composition.

I enjoy my entire house <u>although</u> the kitchen is my favorite room.

Mom clears the garage <u>when</u> it rains so that we can play in it.

UNIT 7: INVENTIVE WRITING

Vocabulary Practice

Listen to someone read the vocabulary words for Lesson 28 aloud.

Speak them aloud yourself.

Read the definitions and sample sentences on the vocabulary cards.

Write the part of speech and the definition beside the word.

comfortable

adjective; making life easy and pleasant

spacious

adjective; containing a large area

Think about the words. Can you use them in your composition?

Lesson 28: My House, Part 2

Unit 7 Composition Checklist
Lesson 28: My House

Inventive Writing

Name: _____

STRUCTURE
- ☐ name and date in upper left-hand corner _____ 2 pts
- ☐ composition double-spaced _____ 3 pts
- ☐ title centered and repeats 1–3 key words from final sentence _____ 5 pts
- ☐ topic-clincher sentences repeat or reflect 2–3 key words (highlight or bold) _____ 10 pts
- ☐ checklist on top, final draft, rough draft, key word outline _____ 4 pts

STYLE

¶1 ¶2 **Dress-Ups** (underline one of each) (3 pts each)
- ☐ ☐ -ly adverb _____ 6 pts
- ☐ ☐ *who/which* clause _____ 6 pts
- ☐ ☐ strong verb _____ 6 pts
- ☐ ☐ *because* clause _____ 6 pts
- ☐ ☐ quality adjective _____ 6 pts
- ☐ ☐ *www.asia* clause _____ 6 pts

CHECK FOR BANNED WORDS (-1 pt for each use):
say/said, see/saw, go/went, good, bad _____ pts

MECHANICS
- ☐ capitalization _____ 10 pts
- ☐ end marks and punctuation _____ 10 pts
- ☐ complete sentences _____ 10 pts
- ☐ correct spelling _____ 10 pts

VOCABULARY
- ☐ vocabulary words - label *(voc)* in left margin or after sentence

Total: _____ 100 pts

Custom Total: _____ pts

Checklist

Teachers are free to adjust a checklist by requiring only the stylistic techniques that have become easy, plus one new one. EZ+1

UNIT 7: INVENTIVE WRITING

Intentionally blank so the checklist can be removed.

Lesson 29: My Friend, Part 1

Structure: Unit 7: Inventive Writing
Style: no new style
Subject: my friend

UNIT 7: INVENTIVE WRITING

Lesson 29: My Friend, Part 1

Goals

- to practice the Unit 7 structural model
- to create a KWO from a writing prompt
- to review vocabulary words

Assignment Schedule

Day 1

1. Play a vocabulary game from the Teacher's Manual.
2. Read Structure Review—Inventive Writing.
3. Read the prompt and complete the practice.
4. Read Notes from the Brain.

Day 2

1. Write a KWO about topic A, one thing you do with your friend.
2. Test your KWO and write a topic sentence.

Day 3

1. Complete Vocabulary Review.
2. Write a KWO about topic B, another thing you do with this same friend.
3. Test your KWO and write a topic sentence.

Day 4

1. Study for Vocabulary Quiz 6. It will cover words from Lessons 25–28.
2. After practicing, use your KWO to give an oral report to a friend or family member. Read. Think. Look up. Speak.

Unit 7

In this lesson students continue to practice asking good questions to generate information for the KWO.

Remember to be patient with yourself and your student. This is a practicable skill that will take time to master.

Remind students that the subject is the thing the entire paper is about. The topic is the division of or thing within the subject. In the last assignment the subject *house* was assigned. In this assignment students must choose a subject (a specific friend) to write about. A friend could be a sibling, cousin, neighbor, or classmate.

Structure Review

Inventive Writing

In Unit 7 your entire composition should be about one subject. Once you know what the subject of the composition is, you determine how many paragraphs to write. Once you know the number of paragraphs, you determine the topics. Each paragraph equals one topic.

2 topics = 2 paragraphs

Subject
- I. Topic A — topic, 5–6 details, clincher
- II. Topic B — topic, 5–6 details, clincher

Prompt

Write two paragraphs about one of your friends.

Subjects and Topics

The topic line follows the pattern *subject, topic,* one more word *about the topic*.

In the sample *Anna* is the subject. *Topic A* is play, and *topic B* is build.

Each topic becomes one paragraph.

Practice

The first thing you must do is decide is who you will write about. Write the names of three friends you know. Choose one. This is the subject of your paper.

(Anna)   Claire   Timmy

Because you must write two paragraphs about your friend, you will choose two topics. Write down four different things you do with this friend. Choose two.

bake   (play)

(build)   swim

The topic sentence will tell the topic of the paragraph. On the KWO write the subject and topic next to the Roman numeral. Follow this pattern.

I. *subject, topic* A   II. *subject, topic* B

Lesson 29: My Friend, Part 1

Notes from the Brain

You will write this paper without the help of source texts. Just like the other assignments, you must begin by writing a KWO.

To write the KWO, take notes from your brain. To do this, ask yourself questions. Use your answers to create the KWO.

who? what? when?
where? why? how?

Describe the topic by asking yourself questions.

Who are we with?

What do we do before we do this?

What do we do after we do this?

When do my friend and I do this?

Where do we do this?

Why do we do this?

How do we feel when we do this?

Draw a picture of something you do with your friend.

The answers to your questions become the details for the outline. As you answer a question, write two or three key words on the KWO. Use symbols, numbers, and abbreviations when possible.

You do not have to answer every question. You do not need to ask the questions in the order they are written. Keep your answers short. You can add more details when you write your composition.

Repeat this process for the second topic.

2 topics = 2 paragraphs

UNIT 7: INVENTIVE WRITING

The topic line follows the pattern *subject, topic,* one more word *about the topic.*

Because the topics for this lesson will probably be verbs, the one more word about the topic will likely be a noun. That is okay. Encourage students to list details related to both words, i.e. play backyard or build Legos™.

The key to the inventive writing process is asking questions. Here are the questions asked that resulted in the sample KWO.

Topic

Who is the subject? *(Anna)*

What do you do with Anna? *(play)*

Where do you play? *(backyard)*

Details

1. When do you play and who else do you play with?
2–3. What do you do?
4–5. What else do you do?
6. How do you feel about your friend?

Clincher

Discuss ideas for a clincher sentence using two or three key words that repeat or reflect words written on the topic sentence line.

Here is a sample clincher sentence:

*I like to **play** with **Anna** in the **backyard**.*

Sample

UNIT 7: INVENTIVE WRITING

Key Word Outline

Next to the Roman numeral (the topic line), write the subject and topic. Follow this pattern: *subject, topic* A. Think of one word to describe the thing you do with your friend. Add this + *word* to the topic line.

Write five or six details about the topic.

I. Topic: *Anna, play, backyard*

1. *afternoons, weekends, w/ siblings* — who?
2. *basket, fishing pole* — what?
3. *gather, wildflowers, hills* — when?
4. *wade, creek, 👀, worms, 🐟* — where?
5. *talk, laugh, splash* — why?
(6.) *☺, relax, best, friend* — how?

Clincher

Test your KWO. For the clincher, repeat or reflect the words on the topic line.

Topic Sentence

The topic sentence tells what the paragraph is about. Use the key words on the topic line (or synonyms of those words) to write a topic sentence.

*I **play** with my friend **Anna** in my **backyard**.*

Sample

Key Word Outline

Next to the Roman numeral (the topic line), write the subject and topic. Follow this pattern: *subject, topic* B. Think of one word to describe the thing you do with your friend. Add this + *word* to the topic line.

Write five or six details about the topic.

II. Topic: _____Anna, build, Legos™_____

    1. _____Anna, invite, 2x week_____ who?

    2. _____bricks, base, instructions_____ what?

    3. _____choose, follow, steps_____ when?

    4. _____sort, think, together_____ where?

    5. _____create, build, hours_____ why?

   (6.) _____picture, show, parents_____ how?

    Clincher

Test your KWO. For the clincher, repeat or reflect the words on the topic line.

Topic Sentence

The topic sentence tells what the paragraph is about. Use the key words on the topic line (or synonyms of those words) to write a topic sentence.

    *I enjoy **building Legos™** with **Anna**.*

Topic

Who is the subject? *(Anna)*

What is another thing you do with Anna? *(build)*

What do you build? *(Legos™)*

Details

1. When do you build?

2–3. How do you build?

4–5. How else do you build?

6. What do you do with what you build?

Clincher

Discuss ideas for a clincher sentence using two or three key words that repeat or reflect words written on the topic sentence line.

Here is a sample clincher sentence:

Anna and I have **built** many **Lego**™ creations.

UNIT 7: INVENTIVE WRITING

Vocabulary Review

Listen to someone read the vocabulary words for Lessons 25–28 aloud.

Speak them aloud yourself.

Read the definitions and sample sentences on the vocabulary cards.

Write the words that match the definitions.

design — to create a plan and drawing for a specific purpose

expel — to force someone to leave a place

store — to put something in a place where it is available

spacious — containing a large area

bond — to form a close relationship with someone

comfortable — making life easy and pleasant

illegal — not allowed by law

desire — to strongly wish for something

Think about the words and their meanings. Which vocabulary words could you use in your composition?

design, spacious, bond

Lesson 30: My Friend, Part 2

Structure: Unit 7: Inventive Writing
Style: no new style
Subject: my friend

UNIT 7: INVENTIVE WRITING

Lesson 30: My Friend, Part 2

Goals

- to write a 2-paragraph composition
- to take Vocabulary Quiz 6

Assignment Schedule

Day 1

1. Play Simplified Jeopardy.
2. Take Vocabulary Quiz 6.
3. Complete Style Practice.

Day 2

1. Say the topic-clincher rule.
2. Write a rough draft for your first paragraph.
3. Highlight or bold the key words *subject, topic A, + word* in the topic and clincher sentences.

Day 3

1. Write a rough draft for your second paragraph.
2. Highlight or bold the key words *subject, topic B, + word* in the topic and clincher sentences.
3. Look at the checklist. Check each box as you complete each requirement.
4. Turn in your rough draft to your editor with the completed checklist attached.

Day 4

1. Draw a picture to put with your composition.
2. Write or type a final draft.
3. Paperclip the checklist, picture, final draft, rough draft, and KWO together.

Unit 7

In this lesson students use the KWO created in Lesson 29 to write two paragraphs about their friend.

Students should follow the topic-clincher rule as practiced and modeled on pages 210–211.

UNIT 7: INVENTIVE WRITING

Style Practice

Strong Verb Dress-Up and -ly Adverb Dress-Up

Look at your KWO and write ideas for each.

Suggested Answers

The suggested answers work with the sample KWO.

Students' answers will depend upon chosen topics.

1. List strong verbs and -ly adverbs to include in your first paragraph.

   strong verbs *wade, hook, catch*

   -ly adverbs *carefully, gently, excitedly*

2. List strong verbs and -ly adverbs to include in your second paragraph.

   strong verbs *design, decide, display*

   -ly adverbs *skillfully, thoughtfully, proudly*

Quality Adjective Dress-Up

Look at your KWO and list two different nouns that you could use in your composition. Next to each noun, write ideas for adjectives that create a strong image and feeling. Avoid banned adjectives.

1. *Anna* *friendly, loyal, generous*

2. *bricks* *colorful, tiny, unique*

Who/Which Clause Dress-Up

Write two sentences with a *who/which* clause that you could use in your composition.

Anna, <u>who</u> carries the fishing pole, walks with me to the creek.

We sort the bricks, <u>which</u> are scattered all over the floor.

Because Clause Dress-Up

Write two sentences with a *because* clause that you could use in your composition.

I like to spend time with Anna <u>because</u> she is my best friend.

We take pictures of our creations <u>because</u> we want to remember them.

www.asia Clause Dress-Up

Write two sentences with a *www.asia* clause that you could use in your composition.

Anna and I run to the meadow <u>where</u> the wildflowers grow.

We follow the instructions <u>if</u> we decide to build a boxed set.

UNIT 7: INVENTIVE WRITING

Lesson 30: My Friend, Part 2

Unit 7 Composition Checklist
Lesson 30: My Friend

Inventive Writing

Name: _____

STRUCTURE

- ☐ name and date in upper left-hand corner — 2 pts
- ☐ composition double-spaced — 3 pts
- ☐ title centered and repeats 1–3 key words from final sentence — 5 pts
- ☐ topic-clincher sentences repeat or reflect 2–3 key words (highlight or bold) — 10 pts
- ☐ checklist on top, final draft, rough draft, key word outline — 4 pts

STYLE

¶1 ¶2 **Dress-Ups** (underline one of each) (3 pts each)

- ☐ ☐ *-ly* adverb — 6 pts
- ☐ ☐ *who/which* clause — 6 pts
- ☐ ☐ strong verb — 6 pts
- ☐ ☐ *because* clause — 6 pts
- ☐ ☐ quality adjective — 6 pts
- ☐ ☐ *www.asia* clause — 6 pts

CHECK FOR BANNED WORDS (-1 pt for each use):
say/said, see/saw, go/went, good, bad _____ pts

MECHANICS

- ☐ capitalization — 10 pts
- ☐ end marks and punctuation — 10 pts
- ☐ complete sentences — 10 pts
- ☐ correct spelling — 10 pts

VOCABULARY

- ☐ vocabulary words - label *(voc)* in left margin or after sentence

Total: _____ 100 pts

Custom Total: _____ pts

Checklist

Teachers are free to adjust a checklist by requiring only the stylistic techniques that have become easy, plus one new one. EZ+1

Intentionally blank so the checklist can be removed.

Contents

Appendices
    I.   Adding Literature.. 221
    II.   Mechanics... 223
    III. Vocabulary.. 225
    IV. Review Games (Teacher's Manual only).. 241

APPENDICES

Appendix I: Adding Literature

Great literature will be a valuable addition to these lessons. Many of these titles have not been reviewed by the Institute for Excellence in Writing. These selections are provided simply to assist you in your own research for books that may be used to supplement this writing curriculum. Teachers should read the books before assigning them to their students.

September

    Excerpts from *Aladdin and Other Favorite Arabian Nights Stories* by Philip Smith
        Aladdin and the Wonderful Lamp
        Ali Baba and the Forty Thieves

    Benjamin Franklin by Ingri and Edgar Parin d'Aulaire

    Start *Black Beauty* by Anna Sewell

October

    Finish *Black Beauty* by Anna Sewell

    Excerpts from *What Your Third Grader Needs to Know* by E.D. Hirsch Jr.
        Androcles and the Lion
        Horatius at the Bridge

    Excerpts from *Classic Myths to Read Aloud* by William F. Russell
        Cupid and Psyche
        Damon and Pythias
        Jason and the Golden Fleece
        Perseus and the Gorgon's Head
        The Sword of Damocles
        The Wanderings of Aeneas

APPENDICES

November

Excerpts from *D'Aulaires' Book of Norse Myths* by Ingri and Edgar Parin d'Aulaire
Introduction
Asgard and the Aesir Gods
The Death of Balder
Odin, the All-father
Thor, the Thunder-god
The Valkyries and Valhalla
The Theft of Thor's Hammer

Start *The Princess and the Goblin* by George MacDonald, abridged by Oliver Hunkin

December

Finish *The Princess and the Goblin* by George MacDonald, abridged by Oliver Hunkin

January

Excerpts from *What Your Third Grader Needs to Know* by E.D. Hirsch Jr.
The Hunting of the Great Bear

Start *Farmer Boy* by Laura Ingalls Wilder

February

Finish *Farmer Boy* by Laura Ingalls Wilder

March

Excerpts from *What Your Third Grader Needs to Know* by E.D. Hirsch Jr.
Gone Is Gone
The People Could Fly

April

Excerpts from *What Your Third Grader Needs to Know* by E.D. Hirsch Jr.
Three Words of Wisdom
William Tell
The Little Match Girl

May

Excerpts from *The Jungle Book* by Rudyard Kipling
Mowgli's Brothers
Kaa's Hunting
Tiger! Tiger!
Rikki-Tikki-Tavi

Appendix II: Mechanics

Well-written compositions are not only written with structure and style, but they also contain correctly spelled words and proper punctuation. This list represents all of the directions that address correct mechanics or writing which are included within various lessons.

Numbers

Use number words and numerals correctly.

Words	numbers expressed in one or two words	*twenty, fifty-three*
	ordinal numbers	*first, second, third*
Numerals	numbers that use three or more words	*123 204*
	numbers mixed with symbols	*$500 40%*
	dates (Do not include st, nd, rd, or th.)	*AD 80* *January 1, 1950*

Capitalization

Capitalize proper nouns and adjectives.

> The Nile River is a river in Africa.

> The hoplite was a foot soldier in the Roman army.

Names

The first time you write a name, write the first and last name. After the first time, write the first and last name or only the last name.

> Benjamin Franklin attached a key to his kite. (first mention)

> When Franklin touched the key, he felt an electric shock. (second mention)

Adventures in Writing: Student Book

APPENDICES

Contractions

Contractions are not used in academic writing.

> The Romans didn't expect Hannibal to cross the Alps. (incorrect)

> The Romans did not expect Hannibal to cross the Alps. (correct)

Dates, Locations, Directions

When a date includes the month, day, and year, place a comma between the day and year. If the date is placed in the middle of a sentence, place a comma on both sides of the year.

> Gli died on June 11, 2020, and is buried in the garden.

Place a comma between a city and state. If the city and state are placed in the middle of a sentence, place a comma on both sides of the state.

> John Muir went to Glacier Bay, Alaska, three times.

Capitalize *north*, *south*, *east*, and *west* when they refer to a region or proper name. Do not capitalize these words when they indicate direction.

> Leif Eriksson was the first European to reach North America.

> Philadelphia streets ran north and south or east and west.

Titles

Italicize names of ships. If a report is handwritten, underline the ship name.

> The *Mayflower* was a small ship.

Capitalize titles that come directly before a name or a country.

> The king owed a debt to Sir William Penn. (title precedes name)

> The King of England gave land to William Penn. (title precedes country)

Appendix III: Vocabulary

Vocabulary cards are found on the blue page as a PDF download. Print them, cut them out, and place them in a plastic bag or pencil pouch for easy reference. Plan to study the words for the current lesson and continue to review words from previous lessons. Try to use the vocabulary words in your compositions. For this purpose, you may use any of the words, even from lessons you have not yet had if you would like to look ahead.

For convenience, the following chart shows the words that go with each lesson and where quizzes fall. Quizzes can be found after the chart. Teachers who do not want students to see the quizzes ahead of time may ask you to tear them from your books and turn them in at the beginning of the school year. This is at the discretion of your teacher.

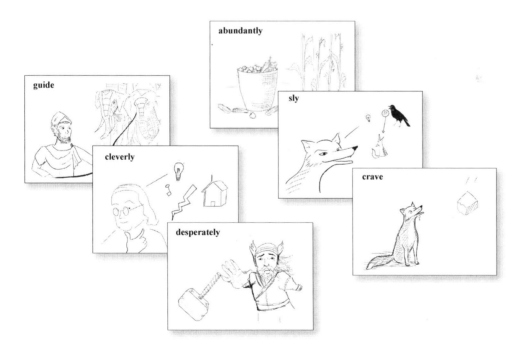

APPENDICES

Vocabulary at a Glance

Lesson 1	dwell	verb	to live; to inhabit
	vast	adjective	very great in size
Lesson 2	organized	adjective	arranged or planned in an effective way
	sprint	verb	to run very fast for a short distance
Lesson 3	melodious	adjective	sweet-sounding
	observe	verb	to watch carefully
Quiz 1			No new words for Lesson 4
Lesson 5	abruptly	adverb	very suddenly and unexpectedly
	forcefully	adverb	with great strength; powerfully
Lesson 6	cautiously	adverb	carefully avoiding danger or risk
	cleverly	adverb	showing intelligent thinking
Lesson 7	guide	verb	to lead in a certain path
	terrified	adjective	extremely afraid
Lesson 8	crave	verb	to desire strongly
	sly	adjective	clever in a dishonest way
Quiz 2			No new words for Lesson 9
Lesson 10	desperately	adverb	showing an urgent need or desire
	vanish	verb	to disappear
Lesson 11	deceive	verb	to make someone believe something that is not true
	declare	verb	to state in a strong and confident way
Lesson 12	abundantly	adverb	richly supplied
	notice	verb	to become aware of
Lesson 13	colossal	adjective	great in size; huge
	proudly	adverb	with pleasure or satisfaction from doing something
Quiz 3			No new words for Lesson 14

Appendix III

Lesson 15	effortlessly	adverb	easily
	metallic	adjective	made of or containing metal
Lesson 16	mottled	adjective	marked with colored spots or areas
	tussle	verb	to fight or struggle roughly
Lesson 17	commotion	noun	noisy excitement and confusion
	slumber	verb	to sleep
Lesson 18	din	noun	a loud, confusing noise
	peacefully	adverb	calmly or quietly; without noise or excitement
Quiz 4			No new words for Lesson 19
Lesson 20	delicate	adjective	easily damaged
	discover	verb	to find
Lesson 21	skilled	adjective	trained or experienced to do something well
	weir	noun	a small dam in a river or stream
Lesson 22	construct	verb	to build or make something
	nutritious	adjective	promoting good health and growth
Lesson 23	cramped	adjective	too small and crowded
	shiver	verb	to shake or tremble with cold, fear, or excitement
Quiz 5			No new words for Lesson 24
Lesson 25	expel	verb	to force someone to leave a place
	illegal	adjective	not allowed by law
Lesson 26	design	verb	to create a plan and drawing for a specific purpose
	desire	verb	to strongly wish for something
Lesson 27	bond	verb	to form a close relationship with someone
	store	verb	to put something in a place where it is available
Lesson 28	comfortable	adjective	making life easy and pleasant
	spacious	adjective	containing a large area
Quiz 6			No new words for Lessons 29 or 30

Adventures in Writing: Student Book

APPENDICES

Appendix III

Vocabulary Quiz 1

| dwell | observe | sprint |
| melodious | organized | vast |

Fill in the blanks with the appropriate word. Be sure to spell correctly.

1. to watch carefully   1. *observe*

2. very great in size   2. *vast*

3. to live; to inhabit   3. *dwell*

4. to run very fast for a short distance   4. *sprint*

5. sweet-sounding   5. *melodious*

6. arranged or planned in an effective way   6. *organized*

Adventures in Writing: Student Book

APPENDICES

Appendix III

Vocabulary Quiz 2

| abruptly | cleverly | forcefully | sly |
| cautiously | crave | guide | terrified |

Fill in the blanks with the appropriate word. Be sure to spell correctly.

1. to desire strongly   1. *crave*

2. clever in a dishonest way   2. *sly*

3. very suddenly and unexpectedly   3. *abruptly*

4. to lead in a certain path   4. *guide*

5. extremely afraid   5. *terrified*

6. carefully avoiding danger or risk   6. *cautiously*

7. with great strength; powerfully   7. *forcefully*

8. showing intelligent thinking   8. *cleverly*

Adventures in Writing: Student Book

APPENDICES

Appendix III

Vocabulary Quiz 3

| abundantly | deceive | desperately | proudly |
| colossal | declare | notice | vanish |

Fill in the blanks with the appropriate word. Be sure to spell correctly.

1. great in size; huge   1. *colossal*

2. to become aware of   2. *notice*

3. to disappear   3. *vanish*

4. richly supplied   4. *abundantly*

5. with pleasure or satisfaction from doing something   5. *proudly*

6. to make someone believe something that is not true   6. *deceive*

7. to state in a strong and confident way   7. *declare*

8. showing an urgent need or desire   8. *desperately*

Adventures in Writing: Student Book

APPENDICES

Vocabulary Quiz 4

| commotion | effortlessly | mottled | slumber |
| din | metallic | peacefully | tussle |

Fill in the blanks with the appropriate word. Be sure to spell correctly.

1. calmly or quietly; without noise or excitement
2. to fight or struggle roughly
3. a loud, confusing noise
4. marked with colored spots or areas
5. noisy excitement and confusion
6. made of or containing metal
7. to sleep
8. easily

1. *peacefully*
2. *tussle*
3. *din*
4. *mottled*
5. *commotion*
6. *metallic*
7. *slumber*
8. *effortlessly*

APPENDICES

Vocabulary Quiz 5

| construct | delicate | nutritious | skilled |
| cramped | discover | shiver | weir |

Fill in the blanks with the appropriate word. Be sure to spell correctly.

1. too small and crowded 1. *cramped*

2. trained or experienced to do something well 2. *skilled*

3. a small dam in a river or stream 3. *weir*

4. to build or make something 4. *construct*

5. promoting good health and growth 5. *nutritious*

6. to shake or tremble with cold, fear, or excitement 6. *shiver*

7. easily damaged 7. *delicate*

8. to find 8. *discover*

Adventures in Writing: Student Book

APPENDICES

Appendix III

Vocabulary Quiz 6

| bond | design | expel | spacious |
| comfortable | desire | illegal | store |

Fill in the blanks with the appropriate word. Be sure to spell correctly.

1. to force someone to leave a place —— 1. *expel*

2. to put something in a place where it is available —— 2. *store*

3. to create a plan and drawing for a specific purpose —— 3. *design*

4. to form a close relationship with someone —— 4. *bond*

5. containing a large area —— 5. *spacious*

6. not allowed by law —— 6. *illegal*

7. to strongly wish for something —— 7. *desire*

8. making life easy and pleasant —— 8. *comfortable*

Adventures in Writing: Student Book

Appendix IV: Review Games

Earning Tickets for the Auction (a semester-long game)

Gather

raffle tickets (5-, 10-, 25-point tickets printed on colored paper)

Play

Because positive reinforcement is a wonderful motivator, throughout the year allow students opportunities to earn tickets that they can use at an auction conducted at the end of each semester. Give tickets when students win games or incorporate vocabulary words and when they do something particularly well. Periodically offer contests for tickets such as "Best Title" or the best of each type of dress-up. Many of the games explained in this appendix include directions for giving tickets.

The Auction (a game to play the last day of each semester)

Gather

items for auction
a whiteboard and marker
an envelope for each student

Prepare

At the end of the semester, ask students to bring one to three items to auction to class. The items can be new or items from home. Students put their tickets in envelopes. Label each envelope with the student name and number of tickets. Write the students' names and number of tickets on a whiteboard in order from greatest to least. Instead of having students physically use tickets when they buy and sell, add and subtract from the totals written on the board.

Play

1. To begin the bidding, ask the student with the most tickets which item he or she would like to be auctioned first. Bids must begin at 25 tickets or higher. Students who would like the item continue to bid. The highest bidder receives the item, and the bid price is subtracted from his or her ticket total. Once a student has purchased an item, he or she may not bid on another item until everyone has bought one item.

2. Repeat this process. Let the second student listed on the board choose the next item. Then let the third student choose, and so forth. This means the last person will get his or her pick of what is left for 25 tickets.

3. Once everyone has one item, it is open bidding for what is left.

Vocabulary Find the Card

Gather

twelve to sixteen index cards with vocabulary words written on each
a timer
pocket chart (optional for large class)

Play

1. Divide the class into three teams and spread the cards face up on a table. In a large class, display the cards in a pocket chart instead of laying on a table. Allow the students thirty seconds to study the cards.

2. Turn the cards face down.

3. Read the definition of one of the words. The first team must turn over one of the word cards, trying to find the word that matches the definition.

    ✔ If the word matches the definition, that team receives two points, and the word card is returned to its spot on the table (face down) so that all word cards remain on the table the entire game. Play continues with the next team and the next definition.

    ✔ If the word card does not match the definition, the word card is returned, and the next team attempts to find the correct word for the same definition. Now the correct word is worth three points. If missed again, the next team tries to find the correct word for the same definition for four points. Continue in this way until the correct word is found. Limit the point value to ten. ***Variation***: When an incorrect word is turned over, award one point if the team that picked it can give its correct definition.

4. After the first word is found, repeat #3 with a new definition. Continue the process until all definitions have been used.

5. The player or team with the most points wins.

Around the World

Gather

vocabulary cards
tickets

Play

1. Start with two students. Read a definition. The first to shout the correct vocabulary word receives a ticket and moves on to challenge the next student.

2. Continue in the same way. The winner always moves on to the next student. If one student makes it all the way "around the world" (beats everyone in the class), he receives 5 extra tickets.

Build-a-Man

Gather

a whiteboard and marker
a die (optional)
tickets

Play

1. Choose a phrase and place lines to represent the letters of the phrase on the board. The phrase may be a vocabulary definition or an IEW concept.

   Example Phrase

   > To remind students what can be written on a key word outline, use the phrase THREE KEY WORDS. On a whiteboard, write a blank for each letter in the phrase.
   >
   > __ __ __ __ __   __ __ __   __ __ __ __ __

2. Students take turns guessing letters, one letter per turn. If the letter is in the puzzle, place it on the correct blank(s) and give the student a ticket for each time it is used. If the letter is not in the puzzle, write it on the bottom of the whiteboard so no one else will guess it. *Variation*: Let students roll a die and give tickets equal to the number rolled times how many times the letter is used.

3. When a student knows the phrase, he or she may solve the puzzle. It does not have to be his turn. If a student states the phrase correctly, he receives 10 tickets.

4. After a student states the phrase, ask a bonus question about the phrase. If the student answers the bonus question correctly, he receives 5 additional tickets.

   Example Question

   > In addition to two to three key words, what may you write on each line of a KWO?
   >
   > *symbols, numbers, and abbreviations*

5. Repeat with several puzzles.

Vocabulary Pictionary

Gather

two whiteboards (or one large one with a line sectioning it)
two whiteboard markers
a die

Play

1. Divide the class into two teams. Assign each a whiteboard. Call one person from each team to the front of the class. Have each drawer roll the die to determine the number of points his or her team will receive if he or she wins the round. Instruct the drawers to write the number rolled on the top of the whiteboards so it is not forgotten.

2. Show the drawers the vocabulary word you want them to draw. They will both draw the same word. Letters and numbers may not be used.

3. The first team to guess the word receives the number of points rolled on the die. Erase the boards and play again with two new drawers.

Elimination

Gather

vocabulary cards
tickets

Play

1. Divide the class into groups of three or four students. Try to have an even number of groups.

2. Begin with the first group. Read a definition of a vocabulary word. The first student in that group to shout out the matching word gets a ticket. Continue with the first group until one student has 3 tickets. He or she is the winner and will advance. The rest of the group has been eliminated.

3. Repeat the process with the other groups.

4. Divide winners into two groups and repeat the process with both groups.

5. Finally, repeat the process with the two remaining students. The winner of the final round receives 5 additional tickets.

Vocabulary Lightning

Gather

vocabulary cards
a timer

Play

1. Divide the class into two or three teams.

2. Choose one or two players from one of the teams to represent the team. Show the representative(s) the stack of vocabulary cards with the word sides up. He or she may not look at the back of the card to see the definition.

3. The representative(s) tries to get the team to say as many of the vocabulary words as possible in one minute. To do so, he or she looks at the first word and gives the team various clues by stating the definition, acting out the word, or describing the picture on the card. He or she may not say things such as what letter the word begins with or what it rhymes with. *Variation:* Do not allow talking—only acting.

4. As soon as someone from the team shouts the correct word, the teacher should place the card on a table and move to the next word. If the representative gets stuck on a word, he or she may "pass" it, resulting in losing a point. For ease in sorting, passed word cards should be placed in a separate stack from the word cards guessed correctly.

5. When the time is up, count the number of words the first team guessed. Subtract the number of words passed. That difference is that team's score for that round. Let other team(s) have a turn in the same way. The team with the highest score wins that round.

6. Play several rounds.

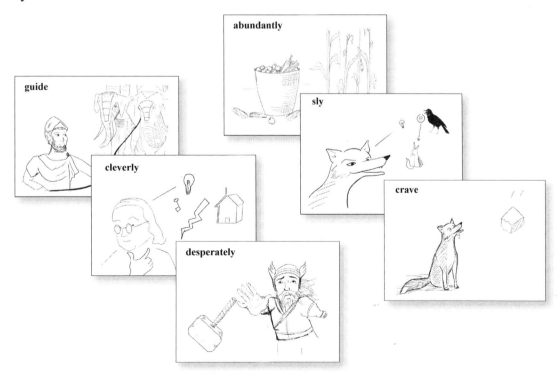

Question Game

Gather

a whiteboard and marker
a die
a list of questions (See suggested questions on pages 250–251.)
tickets

Play

1. Write numbers 1 through how many questions you will be using on a whiteboard and divide the class into three teams.

2. The first team chooses a number, and you read the corresponding question from your list.

   ✔ If the team answers correctly, one of the members rolls the die for points, and you erase the number from the board so that question will not be chosen again.

   ✔ If the team answers incorrectly, you circle the number. That team receives no points, and another team may choose that circled number for double points on their turn.

   Three different ways to roll the die for points:

    The simple way is to roll the die once and receive the points indicated.

    A more challenging way is to let a team roll as many times as they choose, adding each roll to their total for that turn. So, if their first roll is a 4, and then they roll a 3, they are at 7 points. However, if they roll a 6 before they choose to stop rolling, they lose all the accumulated points for that turn. In other words, they must choose after each roll whether to roll again for more points or to stop before they roll a 6.

    As added fun, declare 2 means "Lose a turn" and 4 means "Free roll."

3. Play until most questions have been chosen and teams have had an equal number of turns. Each player on the team with the most points receives 5 tickets.

Tic-Tac-Toe

Gather

a list of questions (See suggested questions on pages 250–251.)
a whiteboard and marker
two dice

Prepare

Draw a Tic-Tac-Toe board and number the squares 1–9.
Write the Special Moves on the whiteboard.

1	2	3
4	5	6
7	8	9

Special Moves

A total of 7	=	Take an extra turn.
Double 1, 2, or 3	=	Erase an opponent's mark.
Double 4, 5	=	Erase an opponent's mark and replace it with yours.
Double 6	=	WILD. Go anywhere. You may erase your opponent's mark if need be.

Play

1. Divide players into an X team and an O team.

2. The X team begins. Read a question. If the team answers correctly, place an X in the square of choice. The team then rolls two dice to determine whether they make special moves before the O team plays. If the team answers incorrectly, the O team plays.

3. The O team plays.

4. Play until one team has three in a row or all squares are filled.

5. Repeat until one team has won two out of three or three out of five games.

Two Strikes and You're Out

Gather

eleven index cards (Write strong verbs and quality adjectives on each. Include vocabulary words.)
five index cards (Write banned words students know on each, repeating words if necessary.)
tickets

Play

1. Place the cards in a pocket chart and cover them with numbers or lay the cards face down on a table.
2. Divide the class into three teams.
3. Teams take turns picking a card.
   - ✔ If the card chosen is a strong verb or a quality adjective, team members must identify it as such and use it in a sentence. If it is a vocabulary word, they should give the definition. They keep the card.
   - ✔ If the card chosen is a banned word, the team receives a strike. When a team has received two strikes, the team is out and may not take any more turns.
4. Play until two teams have been eliminated. The remaining team wins, and each member receives 10 tickets. In addition, give each player on all teams 5 tickets for each strong verb or quality adjective found.

Find the *www.asia* Clause Starters (a variation of the game above)

Gather

seven index cards with *when, while, where, as, since, if, although* written on each
five index cards with *who, what, why, is, and* written on each
tickets

Play

1. Place the cards in a pocket chart and cover them with numbers or lay the cards face down on a table.
2. Divide the class into three teams.
3. Teams take turns picking a card.
   - ✔ If the card chosen is an adverb clause starter, team members must identify it as such and use it in a sentence. They keep the card.
   - ✔ If the card chosen is not an adverb clause starter, the team receives a strike. When a team has received two strikes, the team is out and may not take any more turns.
4. Play until two teams have been eliminated. The remaining team wins, and each member receives 10 tickets. In addition, give each player on all teams 5 tickets for each *www.asia* clause starter found.

Simplified Jeopardy (an end-of-the-year game)

Gather

prepared cards (See suggested questions on pages 250–251.)
three dice
a whiteboard and marker

Prepare

Write several question index cards. Categorize the questions by *Structure*, *Style*, *Mechanics*, or *Vocabulary*. Rank the questions by level of difficulty (1 = easy; 2 = medium; 3 = difficult). Write a question on one side of each card and the category and level of difficulty on the other side.

Play

1. Lay the cards question side down as illustrated.

STRUCTURE 1	STYLE 1	MECHANICS 1	VOCABULARY 1
STRUCTURE 2	STYLE 2	MECHANICS 2	VOCABULARY 2
STRUCTURE 3	STYLE 3	MECHANICS 3	VOCABULARY 3

2. Divide the class into three teams. Teams take turns choosing a question by category and level of difficulty. If the team chooses a Level 1 (easy) question, they may roll one die to determine its point value. If they choose a Level 2, they roll two dice. If they choose a Level 3, they roll three dice.

    ✔ If the team answers the question correctly, they receive the points indicated on the dice. Keep track of points on the whiteboard.

    ✔ If they do not answer correctly, they do not get any points. The missed card should be placed face up as a jeopardy question. This means another team may choose it when it is their turn. Any team that can answer a previously missed question receives double the point value that they roll with two dice. However, if they miss it, they must subtract the points rolled (not doubled).

3. Jeopardy! If a team rolls a total of 5, the question becomes a jeopardy question. This means that if they miss it, 5 points will be subtracted from their point total. However, if they answer correctly, they receive double points, which will be 10 points.

4. Play until time runs out, ensuring each team has had the same number of questions.

❓ Questions (to use with the question games)

Structure (Note Making and Outlines)

1. What is structure? *(the way that parts of something are arranged or put together)*
2. What does KWO mean? *(key word outline)*
3. How many key words do you place on a KWO line? *(two or three)*
4. What are key words? *(the most important words that tell the main idea)*
5. What can you put on a KWO in addition to key words? *(symbols, numbers, and abbreviations)*
6. How do you test a KWO? *(Read. Think. Look up. Speak.)*

Style (Dress-Ups)

7. What dress-ups have we learned thus far? How should you label them? *(underline)*
8. If you take a *who/which* clause out of a sentence, what should be left? *(a complete sentence)*
9. What does a *who/which* clause do? *(describes the noun it follows)*
10. What are the banned words? *(say/said, see/saw, go/went, good, bad)*
11. Improve this sentence by changing the banned word: *Leif Eriksson saw land. (Answers will vary.)*
12. Improve this sentence by adding a *because* clause: *The rooster crowed. (Answers will vary.)*

Structure (Units 3–4)

13. What is the first paragraph of a Unit 3 Retelling Narrative Stories about? *(characters and setting)*
14. What is the second paragraph of a Unit 3 Retelling Narrative Stories about? *(problem or conflict)*
15. What is the third paragraph of a Unit 3 Retelling Narrative Stories about? *(climax and resolution)*
16. When summarizing a reference, what should each paragraph of a summary report begin with? *(topic sentence)*
17. When summarizing a reference, what should each paragraph of a summary report end with? *(clincher sentence)*
18. What is the topic-clincher rule? *(The topic sentence and the clincher sentence must repeat or reflect two or three key words.)*
19. Do Unit 3 narrative story paragraphs have topic sentences? *(no)*

Questions (to use with the question games)

Structure (Units 5–7)

20. When writing a three-paragraph event description from three pictures, how should you begin each paragraph? *(with the central fact of each picture)*

21. What is the central fact? *(the things you see in the picture)*

22. What is a subject? *(the thing you research)*

23. What is a topic? *(the division or parts of the subject)*

24. If you write two paragraphs, how many topics will you write about? *(two)*

25. If the subject is *house*, what are possible topics? *(kitchen, bedroom, layout, history, location, owners, etc.)*

26. When writing a research report (using more than one source text), after you have your sources, what must you do BEFORE you write KWOs? *(choose topics)*

27. Should each note page for a research report have all the notes from the same source or all the notes for the same topic? *(same topic)*

28. What is a fused outline? *(the outline you make by picking notes from source outlines; it is the outline you use to write your paragraph)*

29. When you must write without a source text (your own thoughts), how can you get ideas for what to write? *(ask yourself questions)*

30. What are the brain-helping questions that can help you ask questions to think of more details to add to your writing? *(who, what, when, where, why, how)*

Mechanics

31. Which numbers should written as numerals? *(numbers that cannot be written in one or two words)*

32. The first time a name is written, write the first and last name. After the first time, what do you write for the name? *(the first and last name or only the last name)*

33. When a date includes the month, day, and year, where do you need a comma? *(between the day and year)*

34. What must be changed if this is a sentence in a report (academic writing): The Romans didn't expect Hannibal to cross the Alps. *(The Romans did not expect Hannibal to cross the Alps.)*

35. Where must commas be placed in this sentence: Muir went to Glacier Bay Alaska three times. *(before and after Alaska: Muir went to Glacier Bay, Alaska, three times.)*

Vocabulary

Use any definition and ask the student to give the vocabulary word.